THE IMMORTAL LOVERS
HELOISE AND ABELARD

THE

Immortal Lovers

HELOISE AND ABELARD

Marjorie Worthington

DOUBLEDAY & COMPANY, INC.
GARDEN CITY, NEW YORK
1960

The author gratefully acknowledges the following permissions from:

Benziger Brothers, Inc., and Burns & Oates Ltd., for Abbot McCann's RULES FROM THE REGLA OF ST. BENEDICT.

Alfred A. Knopf, Inc., for C. K. Scott Moncrieff's translation of THE LETTERS OF ABELARD AND HELOISE.

Viking Press, Inc., for letter from Peter the Venerable to Heloise, Mary Martin McLaughlin's translation in THE PORTABLE MEDIEVAL READER.

Harvard University Press, for excerpts from THE MEDIAEVAL MIND, Henry Osborn Taylor.

The Free Press of Glencoe, Ill., for excerpts from STORY OF MY MISFORTUNES, translated by Henry Adams Bellows.

LIBRARY OF CONGRESS CATALOG CARD NUMBER 60–13751
COPYRIGHT © 1960 BY MARJORIE WORTHINGTON
ALL RIGHTS RESERVED
PRINTED IN THE UNITED STATES OF AMERICA
FIRST EDITION

TO

Dorothy and John K. M. McCaffery,
who introduced me to the nuns of
the Regina Laudis Monastery, in
Bethlehem, Connecticut. For this, and
all their help and encouragement,
my deepest thanks.

94771

THE IMMORTAL LOVERS
HELOISE AND ABELARD

1

It is difficult to separate truth from legend when writing about a man or woman who lived even a generation ago. With people who lived in a world eight hundred and fifty odd years earlier than our own, the task would seem impossible. And yet in some respects it is easier, in that we can see the forest and not the trees.

For Abelard we have his often translated *Historia Calamitatum,* the account of his trials and tribulations, and also a few treatises, glosses, and poems, although there are even some doubts about the authenticity of the poems. For Heloise we have a few letters, including possibly the most beautiful love letters ever written. Otherwise, what is there? A few stones, an illuminated manuscript or two, a handful of dust. The old abbeys kept a careful record, not of the newly born but of the dead, whose bones they preserved as relics to add to their prestige.

And yet, when the dust of the ages is blown away, there remains the story of a man and a woman who knew hope and desire, temptation, pain, sorrow, and joy not too different from our own—except that with Heloise and Abelard those human experiences attained heroic proportions.

Heloise was born at the start of the twelfth century, probably 1100, in France. The details of her birth have remained obscure. Her mother's death was recorded under the name Hersindis in the register of the Paraclete near Troyes. It is said that through Hersindis, Heloise was related to the noble Montmorency family. As for her father, even less is known. It has been said that she was the natural daughter of Fulbert, a canon of Notre Dame, but there is nothing to substantiate this claim, and more authority for the belief that Fulbert was her uncle. Other authorities claim that she was the natural daughter of Hersindis, first abbess of Sainte-Marie-aux-Bois, and of a Montmorency. Some say that Heloise was the daughter of a canon of Paris named Jean—and so it goes. Heloise herself never mentioned her origins, and neither did Abelard.

What we do know for a fact is that she was orphaned at an early age and became the ward of Fulbert, said to be her uncle and only living relative. He was a canon of Notre Dame Cathedral, with secular duties and privileges. As such, he was permitted to maintain his own domicile within the shadow of the cathedral. There is, in fact, a small house still standing today on the Ile de la Cité, which bears the following inscription:

> *Heloise, Abelard, lived here.*
> *Sincere lovers. Precious models.*
> *The year 1118.*

The prospect of taking a girl child to live with him must have displeased the canon not a little. He would, no doubt, have shuddered at the possibility of grubby, sticky little hands soiling his precious books, of which he had many, for Fulbert was a scholar as well as a churchman. And the idea of childish prattle interrupting his meditations as well as his learned conversations with other scholars, must have horrified him.

He did the only sensible thing. He sent Heloise to the convent at Argenteuil to be raised by the nuns, who were much better equipped to take care of her needs than a bachelor such as he. If the child should decide to become a nun, Fulbert probably reasoned, that would answer a great many problems. For how should a young girl with doubtful background and no dowry acquire a husband?

From all the evidence to be found, Heloise seems to have been happy at the convent. She became a favorite of the nuns, who found her not only receptive to their instruction but eager for knowledge and extremely intelligent.

She appears to have been a lovely child, tall for her age and slender, with thick brown hair, large gray eyes, and fine features. She had a gracious manner which endeared her to the nuns, although they may have doubted at times whether her thoughts were sufficiently on heaven and spiritual matters to indicate a real vocation. She had a voracious curiosity about life, and was prone to admire nature—the trees and flowers in the cloister gardens, and the gentle movement of the Seine as it flowed past the walls of the convent. She was a thoughtful child, and the questions she asked the nuns were sometimes difficult to answer.

The town of Argenteuil has grown considerably since the Middle Ages. Now it is a thriving city about five miles from Paris by the Porte de Neuilly. There are several important industries and prospering vineyards. Every autumn, when the grapes are ripe, there is a special fête which brings visitors from Paris and elsewhere. There is a fine boulevard and a market place said to be named for Heloise. But the convent is no more.

In the early part of the twelfth century, only a few houses clustered around the convent, which had been a monastery until Charlemagne turned it into a nunnery for his daughter, Theodrada, who became the first abbess of Argenteuil. Called Ste. Marie, the convent rivaled in power and wealth the royal monastery of St. Denis around the bend in the river. After Charlemagne died, it was destroyed by the Normans who invaded Paris, but was restored by Queen Adelaide at the end of the tenth century and run by Benedictine nuns who increased the original endowment of lands, forests, and vineyards, until Ste. Marie of Argenteuil became one of the richest convents in France.

So it was when Heloise was a boarding student there. But more important to her than the wealth of the convent was the presence of several nuns of culture and erudition. From these she learned of the classical writers: the philosophers, poets, and even the dramatists of Greece and Rome. By the time she was fourteen, it was said, Heloise could not only read Latin and Greek, but could speak those languages as well.

In spite of this exceptional opportunity for improving her mind, there must have been times when a healthy, inquisitive, eager child would have rebelled against the restrictions to her freedom imposed by her environment. Another child might have become hypocritical or openly rebellious, but there is nothing to indicate that Heloise gave the nuns any trouble of this kind. All that is known of those early years is that she applied herself to her studies with astonishing zeal.

She learned her catechism, of course, and recited with the other children:

"*Esprit-Saint, venez en nous, eclairez nos âmes de vos lumières et embrasez nos coeurs de votre divin amour. . . . Mon Dieu, qui êtes present partout, et plus particulièrment dans le lieu de la prière, je vous adore ici de toutes les puissances de mon âme. . . .*"

But, knowing the questioning mind of Heloise, it is possible that even while she was asking the Holy Ghost to appear to her and the other children, and warm their hearts with His presence —while she was telling God she adored Him, who was present everywhere and especially in the place of prayer—she was preparing questions for the nuns which they could not answer.

And, at the same time that she was learning to say, "*Au nom du Père, et du Fils, et du Saint-Esprit. Ainsi soit-il,*" she was reading Lucan and Seneca, as well as the *Lives of the Saints*.

The convents of France in the early twelfth century were of the Benedictine order, which included the Cistercian and Cluniac. (The term convent, incidentally, originally meant the body of persons gathered together in a monastery, from the Latin *conventus*, but it has gradually come to mean a nunnery.) St. Benedict, who founded the order around the year 500, defined a monastery as "a school of the service of the Lord." He established a monastic rule which was used in western Europe for many centuries, and which will be described in greater detail later on. It included the general duties of abbots and monks, the order of worship, penalties for faults, internal administration, reception of guests, conduct of monks when traveling, and rules for admission to the order. This rule applied to convents as well, and of course to Ste. Marie of Argenteuil.

The nun's day was divided as follows: Religious devotions, consisting of night vigils and offices said at the seven canonical hours between dawn and dusk, solitary meditation, reading, manual work, meals, sleep.

Into this regimen were fitted the hours of instruction for the children placed in the nuns' care. How, one wonders, did an active little girl spend her time when not in the schoolroom or at devotions? What of the hours for play? Or the hours for receiving the loving attention that all children need?

Were they permitted to walk along the banks of the Seine —in groups, perhaps, or in columns two by two? Or were they strictly confined within the walls of the convent? How dark it must have been inside those walls, with the narrow windows and high vaulted corridors, and how cold during the long winters of northern France!

Around the cloister, which was an open court, were grouped the chapel, the dormitory, a kitchen, and a refectory. Behind the convent were the gardens and orchards and vineyards; workshops and other small buildings. But the principal divisions of the convent were built around the cloister, and of these the most important were the chapter house, in which all business was conducted, the chapel, and the refectory, where the meals were served.

The dormitory at Argenteuil was on the second floor, over the chapter house, and there were stone stairs down which the nuns could fly for their night vigils and prayers. How often, one wonders, was a little girl awakened during the night by the bells and by the silent forms in their black gowns hastily pulled over the long white chemises? Perhaps she got used to the swift and silent movements, the tinkling bells sounding at intervals during the long cold nights, the voices chanting "Ave Maria, gratia plena" or "Pater Noster," and enjoyed the refreshing sleep of childhood and innocence without waking at all.

Heloise was very young when her mother died, and she probably had few memories to make her homesick. And, however confined she may have felt within the convent walls, there was a way to escape—by means of the wonderful books she had learned to read. The world of the mind, she discovered early, had no limitations, no boundaries.

Studying and teaching in the early Middle Ages were a monopoly of the church and of one social class, consisting of nuns and lay brothers. The language in which they taught was Latin, and the traditional program was the seven liberal arts. The subjects included grammar, rhetoric, and logic, which comprised the *trivium*; arithmetic, geometry, astronomy, and music, which comprised the *quadrivium*. Grammar included not only the usual rules of syntax, but a study of the classical writers: Vergil, Seneca, Horace, etc. Rhetoric included Cicero, and logic included the *Organon* of Aristotle. The authority for the teaching of mathematics was Euclid.

Just how many of these subjects were taught by the nuns of Argenteuil, at the time when Heloise was a student there, we do not know. We have proof, however, that she could quote at ease from the classic writers and that her knowledge of Latin was so thorough that she was able to express her deepest emotions in that tongue. Abelard, writing of her much later, said that Heloise was the only woman of her time to possess a knowledge of Latin, Greek, and Hebrew.

The fame of this small girl's accomplishments spread beyond the convent of Argenteuil. The nuns, proud of their pupil, may have boasted a little to occasional visitors, and these carried the tale along to Paris. For at this time, especially in France, there was a general thirst for knowledge such as had not been felt before, and which increased until it reached its great flowering in the Renaissance.

Feudalism was still in force, but under Louis VI ("The Fat") the relation between serf and overlord was more and more determined by free contract. The cathedrals, and the universities attached to them, were filled with eager young men no longer merely interested in bearing arms or writing songs for unattainable—or not so unattainable—great ladies. And the church was no longer strictly maintaining a gulf between religion and philosophy.

A new art, a new intelluctual culture were coming into being, and Heloise, born at about the time of this general awakening, felt the excitement of it even in the dark classroom of the convent at Argenteuil. Although she may not have realized it then, nothing could have been more fortunate for a female with intellectual aspirations than to have been brought up within the church itself, the fountainhead of all the learning available in her day.

It was inevitable that the gossip about the young paragon at Argenteuil should reach the ears of her uncle Fulbert, who may have forgotten he had a ward to whom he owed at least a perfunctory sign of interest. But now, as he heard her name mentioned by the students at Notre Dame in terms of admiration, his interest and curiosity, if not his conscience, were aroused.

Overcoming any misgivings he may have felt at the intrusion of a young female upon his celibate existence, Fulbert sent a message to the nuns, asking that Heloise be permitted to visit him for a few days or, at the most, a few weeks.

Heloise, according to most authorities, was fourteen years old when she received her uncle's invitation. She knew very little about the outside world. The people she had read about in books belonged to a life that was past. And the only people she had met were the nuns, the lay brothers who assisted them, and the lay servants who did the manual work around the convent.

Paris would be, she knew, very different from this closed world which was the only one she could remember having lived in. Even in the house of a canon of Notre Dame it would be different. There would be young students—young men students —and Heloise had all the curiosity about them natural in an ardent young girl with a vivid imagination.

She may have had, also, a sense of pride because she had an uncle, someone to whom she really belonged, instead of being just another little orphan like most of the children at the convent. It is so terribly important to a child to feel that she belongs to someone—even someone like Fulbert, who had remembered his ward at last and actually wanted to see her.

Whatever reservations the good nuns of Argenteuil may have had about the effect of this visit, brief as it promised to be, upon their prize student, they took pains to warn her against this and that, to polish her table manners, and to provide her with a suitable wardrobe.

The dress of the period was worn over a linen chemise which had a long skirt, reaching to the instep or to the ground, and long, tight sleeves. (A bare arm in a woman was considered shocking.) The neck of the chemise was high, and the material was of fine linen, such as the nuns used for their wimples. It was hand-woven in the neighborhood, and was as durable as it was fine. When it was washed, saffron was added to the water to give it a creamy tint, which was considered more desirable than a dead white. The saffron also had a pleasant smell.

Over the chemise was worn a close tunic with tight sleeves, or a somewhat looser tunic with looser, shorter sleeves, in which case the chemise was visible at the neck and wrists. Sometimes a loose belt was worn, but more for decoration than use, as the tunic usually followed closely the lines of the figure. At the opening of the neck and the sleeves there were lacings. The colors were subdued: dove gray, soft brown, and sometimes blue.

Shoes were of a soft material, and had rounded toes as a rule, though some of the women in town wore pointed toes like the men's and even, in some cases, raised toes that were called "ram's horns." Often the shoes were embroidered in colored silks.

For an outer garment there was a half circular mantle with an embroidered border and a lining of contrasting material. It was often fastened at one shoulder with a silken cord.

When the nuns provided Heloise with her wardrobe for this first visit to Paris, they may have added a purse to hang from her belt, and perhaps they put a few coins of the realm in it. It was her first worldly possession, making her feel as if she already belonged to that strange outside world, where so much that she had accepted as gifts from God had to be bought, sold, or in some way earned.

Argenteuil was not far from Paris, but it was a half day's journey for Heloise, seated on a horse behind her uncle's servant. She was a little sad after saying good-by to the nuns, but as the morning wore on and new sights came before her eyes, she lost any feeling of sadness. With each hoofbeat on the cobbles, her heart beat faster and faster. She thought that, if she pleased her uncle, he might let her stay with him for a long time, perhaps —who knew?—forever.

It was, in fact, to be a number of years before she traveled the road back to Argenteuil, and almost all that could happen to a woman was compressed into that short time, leaving her with only a single direction and a single purpose that were almost, but never entirely, holy.

2

The Paris that Heloise approached in the year 1114 was scarcely more than an overgrown hamlet. The low buildings were shabbily constructed, the streets were narrow and dirty, with pigs and chickens overrunning the place and feeding on refuse that clogged the gutters. In fact, it is said that the oldest son of King Louis VI was thrown and killed one day, in Paris, when a pig ran between the legs of his horse.

Most of the activity was centered on the Ile de la Cité, because of Notre Dame, which drew merchants over the Grand Pont to attend services and students from the Latin Quarter over the Petit Pont to attend lectures. The cathedral that we know was not built until 1623, but on the same site there was a Romanesque church, the cloisters of which served as classrooms for the growing University of Paris.

It was on the Ile de la Cité that Canon Fulbert lived, in a small house that was, to do it justice, a little less shabby than its neighbors. It even wore, for those days, an air of gentility befitting the residence of a canon of the church. And shabby though the district was, it was the intellectual hub of Europe and a most congenial place for a scholar who lived in his books and liked to bask in the reflected light of the great minds which were drawn to the university.

For in spite of its surface provincialism, shabbiness, and filth, Paris was then, as now, an exciting place to live. The very stones under foot rocked with the changes that were occurring in the social, intellectual, and spiritual life of Europe.

When Louis VI, head of the House of Capet, came to the throne in 1108, France was more or less at the mercy of the feudal barons. The crown's domain was limited to Paris and about eleven other counties. The barons in their castles seemed more powerful than the king.

In his reign, Louis succeeded in strengthening the power of the throne and diminishing the power of the feudal barons. Up to then it had been, one might say, almost embarrassing to be king of France. But now Louis and his principal minister, Suger, Abbot of St. Denis, were making even the roads of France safer for the people and providing hope for millions of vassals and serfs.

Without actually waging war against the overlords, the crown added city to city, fief to fief, and province to province until France became united. One of the ways in which this happened was the weakening of the great barons through their participation in the Crusades. Many had gone off to the Holy Land, leaving debts behind, which the king took care of! Some had returned with their lives and a certain amount of plunder from the countries on their route, but a great many of them were either impoverished by the experience or had not returned at all. Louis VI took advantage of the situation.

He granted charters to towns for self-government, and exempted them from paying taxes to their feudal lords. Commerce began to flourish as soon as the roads became safer, and, what was most important, the common man began to acquire a sense of his own importance.

The Crusades, while they played a great part in the history of the Middle Ages, did not directly affect the lives of Heloise and Abelard. The First Crusade, begun in 1096, when Peter the Hermit returned from the Holy Land with tales of atrocities heaped on Christians by the Saracens, was ended by 1100. The Second Crusade, instigated by St. Bernard of Clairvaux, lasted only from 1147 to 1149. The Third, led by Richard the Lion Hearted, took place between the years 1189 and 1193, by which time the story that concerns us was over.

The Ile de la Cité, with its Romanesque cathedral and its

university, was in the geographical center of all the unrest and movement. And yet it managed to keep itself remote from the sordid aspects of commercialism and politics.

One of the busiest streets through which the students passed, on their way to and from their classes at Notre Dame, was the Rue des Chantres. Since there were no cafe terraces with marble-topped tables at which students could, for the price of a glass of wine or beer, sit and talk for hours, they gathered in the street to discuss philosophy and argue some point or other or, perhaps, to listen to the words of a song written by the most popular of their teachers, Abelard.

Canon Fulbert's house was on this Rue des Chantres. There were fewer pigs running underfoot, but the gutters were filled with ordure, and, under the jutting roofs of neighboring houses, the household linen was hung to dry, as it is hung today in the provincial towns of France and Italy—shamelessly and as a matter of course.

It was to this house that the canon's servant brought Heloise. It isn't hard to imagine what her emotions were when she reached the end of her journey and waited to be received by a member of her own family. At the convent, personal attachments had been frowned upon in favor of complete devotion to God, His Son, and the Virgin Mother. Such devotion could fill the needs of those dedicated women, the nuns, but Heloise was a young girl, and she needed someone nearer to love and be loved by. Her heart was filled with warmth toward this uncle she had never met. She hoped she would please him.

As she stood on the threshold of the narrow house, on the steps that had been built to protect it from the river that flowed close by and on occasion overflowed its banks, Heloise turned to look at the Seine, her old friend, which ran a little faster here than it did at Argenteuil. And the presence of her beloved river helped a little to remove a sense of strangeness. For it would be strange, indeed, to live for a while without rules to guide her like a handrail, as there had been in the convent.

Fulbert's welcome was presumably kind enough. He may have been surprised to see a young girl with her hair done up in a soft

bun, instead of in a braid down her back, and this may have
caused a little awkwardness to come between them at first, since
the bachelor Fulbert rarely entertained women guests.

The tour of his house was brief. On the first floor was the
parlor in which Fulbert had his meals and received his friends.
In the winter he spent most of his time here, to enjoy the heat
from a fireplace built in the center of the room and to save on
heating the rest of the house. The canon was a frugal man.
There was very little furniture—a few oak chests, a long table,
and two or three chairs.

Off the parlor was the little room the canon used as a study
during the milder months of the year. It was in this study that
he kept his precious books, in specially built cupboards. Heloise's
joy at seeing these, her recognition of some of the titles, and her
keen interest and curiosity about those she had not yet read,
pleased her uncle and helped to break the ice of this visit. She
had her first chance to exhibit some of the erudition of which he
had heard, and he had the thrill of showing his prized possessions. Thus a bond of interest was established that was stronger,
perhaps, than any mere relationship of flesh and blood.

On the second floor of the house, running its full length, was
the room that had been made ready for Heloise. There were three
small windows with thick glass, not so opaque but that she
could get a view of the Seine. The ceiling was crossed by tim-
bers that had been painted with bright colors to relieve the
austerity of the heavy oak furnishings. The bed was a couch,
piled with draperies and furs for warmth, and beneath these
were sheets that had been freshly aired for her visit and still
bore a faint smell of saffron from the last washing.

Next to this long room was an even narrower and much
smaller bedroom. This was for the use of any additional guest,
but since Fulbert was not in the habit of extending hospitality
for the night very often, he regarded it as wasted space, and
grumbled about it and the impossibility of keeping the upper
chambers heated, unless he wanted to ruin himself.

As a canon of Notre Dame, Fulbert received a prebend from
the cathedral. Originally this was a daily allowance at meals, but

since canons were now permitted to have their own domiciles, it had become a stipend granted out of the estate of the cathedral which the canon served in a clerical capacity.

Until the tenth century, canons were bound by laws of celibacy and obedience, but after that they became secular. Originally the term canon meant an ecclesiastic residing with others in the chapter house of a cathedral or church. Later it meant one of a number of dignitaries who formed a council to the bishop and were expected to perform certain duties in the cathedral or church. After the tenth century, the communal life of the canons was abandoned. They formed, instead, a body called a chapter, which met at certain intervals for a definite purpose. They thus became secular, since they no longer lived under monastic rule.

Fulbert was attached, but not bound, as were the priests and bishops, to the Cathedral of Notre Dame. He therefore enjoyed certain liberties which the priests and other church dignitaries did not. For instance, he was permitted to eat meat and to wear linen, and, if he liked, he could marry.

Fulbert enjoyed all the liberties to which he was entitled, except the one permitting him to marry. He much preferred the companionship of scholars and his books to the disturbances caused by a woman in the house, whether as a wife or otherwise. It can be understood if he felt ill at ease at the beginning of his niece's visit, and relieved, later, when he discovered that a young woman need not be a nuisance but an enjoyable companion.

What a delightful surprise it was when, that first night at supper, Heloise began asking questions about the books in his library. She mentioned the works she had already read at the convent—the writings of the church fathers, of course, but also Plato and Aristotle. She could discuss, with as much ease and enthusiasm as one of Fulbert's own colleagues, the works of Jerome, Ambrose, Augustine, and Josephus.

When Fulbert asked if she had as yet made the acquaintance of the works of the greatest poet of all, Vergil, Heloise showed so much eagerness to begin reading the *Aeneid* that Fulbert forgot his fears that his precious books might be soiled by a careless female's fingering, and rushed her off to the library to show her his most valued volumes. He promised her that she could read them for as long as she remained in his house.

Who knows, if the canon Fulbert had not owned all twelve books of Vergil's *Aeneid*, or been generous enough to permit a young girl to feast her eyes and soul on them, how long Heloise would have remained in Paris? And, whether, if she had gone back to the convent after the originally planned first week or so were ended, she would ever have meet Abelard? Our destinies seem to hang by such gossamer threads.

So fascinated was Heloise by the story of Dido and Aeneas that she spent day after day at the oak table in her uncle's study, where the light came dimly through a thick pane of glass coated with dust. She had no need to be entertained, as any other young woman would have expected to be, nor did she seem desirous of exploring Paris. It was enough for her to be able to spend the day reading Vergil, and then to join her uncle for the evening meal of meat and fruit, and to discuss with him what she had read.

And when the wine made her uncle sleepy and she could see his head nod, she was content to escape to her big, cold room, and to dream of the lovers whose story so enthralled her. Before this, all that she knew, through her reading, of men and women had been more or less in terms of martyrdom and miracles. Now Vergil was showing her a world peopled by different beings, those who were neither saints nor martyrs.

As the story unfolded, Heloise became more and more lost in amazement and in sympathy for Dido, the proud queen of Carthage who welcomed to her shore the shipwrecked Aeneas and then fell hopelessly in love with him. When Aeneas stole away from Carthage, breaking the queen's heart and impelling her to end her life on a funeral pyre, Heloise wept that life and love could be so cruel to women.

Although she was moved as much by the poet's language and his ideas, it was by this reading of the story of the tragedy of love that the convent child, without realizing it, perhaps, any more than did her uncle, was becoming a young woman and no longer a child.

The visit of Heloise, which was to be so brief, extended to a year and then to two years. When the nuns at Argenteuil sent messengers to ask when the child was to be returned to them, Fulbert sent back vague answers. They must not worry about her studies, he told them, as she was continuing them under his auspices. She seemed content to remain under his roof, and he, though he admitted it still with astonishment, found it extremely pleasant to have her with him.

From time to time, when Fulbert entertained some church dignitaries or distinguished scholars, he would summon Heloise and encourage her to display her knowledge. She was made much of by these learned colleagues, who called her a second Hypatia and paid both her and her uncle many compliments. She would remain in this distinguished company until a sign from Fulbert that she might leave. And it is most likely that she heard the name of Abelard mentioned many times, either in praise or in condemnation—for no one was able to speak of the famous teacher without taking violent sides.

Her imagination was stirred by all that she heard of the master, who was said to be not only a brilliant dialectician but a poet as well—and handsome and charming as a man. His fame had spread all over France—perhaps she had already heard of him in the convent at Argenteuil—so that he was not a complete stranger when she heard him discussed in the house on the Rue des Chantres.

"Was there a town or village," she wrote much later, "but seethed at the word of your coming? What eye but followed you as you went by?"

The cloisters of the Cathedral, where Abelard held his classes, were but a step away. What more probable than that Heloise, her curiosity growing out of bounds, left her uncle's house to mingle with the crowds of students, so that she might see the man himself and hear the golden words he poured forth in a style that had no equal in all of Europe.

The ground for the meeting between Heloise and Abelard had been well prepared before it actually took place.

3

Pierre du Pallet, known as Abelard, was born in the year 1079, in the town of Pallet, about eight miles from the city of Nantes, in the section of France then called Palatium.

His father, Berenger, was the Sieur du Pallet, a landowner called, by some, a nobleman. A château, destroyed in 1420, once dominated the town. A few ruins of the château remain today —several tombs and a stone cross.

Abelard was the oldest son of Berenger and his wife, Lucie. The other children were Raoul, Porcaire, Dagobert, and a daughter, Denise. Their childhood seems to have been an exceptionally happy one.

Berenger, although by necessity a soldier, was less interested in waging war than the other members of his class. He had a deep respect and love for learning, and, when Pierre showed an aptitude for letters instead of the sword, his father encouraged him and provided whatever instruction there was available.

"I being the first born," Abelard wrote, "in so far as I was dearer to him than the rest, so much the more diligently did he care for my education."

Both the Sieur du Pallet and his wife were devout Christians and, along with his other studies, Pierre was given a sound religious instruction. It was not long, however, before the teachers who were hired to instruct the boy in grammer, rhetoric, and mathematics were found inadequate for his demands.

It was an indication of the new wave of spiritual and intellectual fervor of the times to find the oldest son of a Breton family encouraged to become a student. By long tradition, the Bretons had been good warriors—from the time when the Celts of that region, then known as Armorica, tried to withstand their Roman conquerors in the fifth century. After the Romans left, missionaries from Britain and Ireland converted the Bretons to Christianity, but they were still principally occupied by fighting off raiders, including the Norsemen of the ninth century. In the middle of the eleventh century, Breton adventurers fought with William the Conquerer at the Battle of Hastings, and then hurried home to protect their own country against William's attempt to add Brittany to his conquests.

Pierre's brothers were true to the Breton tradition and were interested in little else than the arts of waging war, and yet they made no criticism of their older brother because he preferred his books to the joys of the hunt or the thrilling sport of waging small wars with neighboring barons. Pierre was as strong, if not stronger than they, fully as brave, and could undoubtedly have beaten them all at their games had he chosen to do so.

At the age of seventeen, when Pierre announced to his father that he wished to turn over his inheritance, and the privileges of the first-born to his brother, there was no attempt made to dissuade him. He was sent on his way with his father's blessings and with enough provisions to live on until he should establish himself as a scholar and be able to make his own living.

Thus Pierre Abelard, as he was from then on to call himself, set out for his destination, which was Paris. His intentions were twofold: to search for an abstract thing called truth, and to impress upon the world that Abelard was a scholar it would do well to listen to.

He was in no hurry. Attached to his saddle was a lute, and when he was bored, or inspired, he would compose songs and accompany himself on the strings. For Abelard, in spite of his interest in the science of pure reason, was to be known also as one of the finest poets of his age.

He made several stops, in order to try out certain schools of which he had heard—or rather to try himself on them and on the teachers. He listened but he also spoke, dueling with the masters and coming off victor each time. There was nothing he seemed to enjoy more than stirring up placid pools of academic philosophy. That he made enemies as well as friends along his route concerned him not at all.

If, by the dialectics he adored and of which he was an early master, he twisted the words and thoughts of others to fit his own arguments, that seemed unimportant. People listened when he spoke, and Abelard, who thought highly of himself, having as yet encountered no mind superior to his, enjoyed a good audience.

The schools of France in the Middle Ages belonged, as we know, to the church. It was through the monks, who made more or less faithful copies, by hand, of the great books, that literature managed to survive through the centuries. Almost every cathedral had its school, and many of the abbeys as well. To these schools, students from all over Europe came in great numbers, and mutual rivalries sprang up, sometimes flaring into violence.

Groups of students would choose their masters and follow them from place to place. The custom of exchange professorships that we enjoy today was well established in the twelfth century. Schools were rated according to the fame of their professors. Many of the students were apprentice professors, that is, candidates for mastership. They were subject to long terms of instruction, at the end of which they were to deliver a public lecture. This was known as a "masterpiece," and on it they would be judged if they were fit to become full teachers.

In the time of Abelard, the schools of Chartres and Paris were at the height of their fame and importance. In Paris, the most popular teacher was William of Champeaux, and Abelard decided to attend his classes.

Of this William, Abelard wrote, in his *Historia Calamitatum*, that he was "a man at that time pre-eminent, rightly and by common repute . . . with whom I stayed for a while, welcomed by him at first but afterwards a great burden to him, since I endeavoured to refute certain of his opinions and often ventured to reason with him, and at times showed myself superior to him in debate. Which things, indeed, those who among my fellow students were esteemed the foremost suffered with all the more indignation in that I was junior to them in age and in length of study."

This picture which Abelard gives, himself, of the youth of twenty, harassing the master day after day, and before his own group of students, helps us to understand the man who was later accused not only of arrogance but of heresy, which he may not have deserved. Abelard had a high opinion of himself, but in all fairness it must be acknowledged that he had an even higher regard for what he believed was truth.

In 1100, students and teachers accepted the laws of the church and, since it was permitted, of Aristotle. But it was only in order that, with the help of Aristotle and his syllogisms, they could help to build up the church intellectually.

What occupied the schools at that time was the subject of "universals." The affirmation or denial of the whole of a class, such as: "All men are animals," or "No men are omniscient," could, apparently, lend itself to as many variations as that imaginary subject attributed jestingly to the Middle Ages: "How many angels can stand on the head of a pin?"

It led to a kind of logic that was most easily reduced to absurdity, and was therefore irresistibly fascinating to youthful students, as well as to some minds that were especially acute. By its use it was easy to force an opponent into wild alternatives. Socrates is said to have used this method to discredit his adversaries, and Abelard was the first French master of it.

But as neither the church nor state enjoy being reduced to an absurd position, both Socrates and Abelard were punished. Abelard tried to clarify his position in a gloss discovered only comparatively recently in the libraries of Milan and Lunel. Briefly summarized, the doctrine of universals, according to Abelard, came down to this: that God was the ultimate universal, and that Truth was real—and outside of human experience.

However, at the time that Abelard was a student in the classes of William of Champeaux, he took every opportunity to differ with the master and to make him appear ridiculous before his pupils. It was apparently a game with Abelard, and one which he seemed to enjoy, but from a worldly standpoint it would have been much wiser to let William alone. Abelard was, after all, at this point, merely an adventuresome youth, whereas William of Champeaux was a churchman. Abelard had the support of the other students, as he always had of anyone who came under the spell of his devastating charm—except the conservative members of the church, and they were the most powerful. William had this support, and was accordingly rewarded.

Either because William and his supporters made things too uncomfortable for Abelard at this time, or because Abelard wearied of a game in which he had shown himself superior, the young scholar left Paris for a while and went in search of another school where he might aspire to be master instead of student.

He established himself not far from Paris, at Melun, which at that time was an important town because the king had a residence there. Students flocked to the young master in such numbers that according to Abelard, William of Champeaux became jealous and tried, by many underhanded tricks, to discredit his teaching. This had no other result than to bring discredit upon William and to increase the popularity of Abelard.

In the *Historia Calamitatum*, Abelard wrote, "From this beginning of my school so much did my name in the art of dialectics begin to be magnified that not only the repute of my fellow scholars but that of the master [William] himself, began to decline and was gradually extinguished. Hence it came about that, presuming more largely upon myself, I made haste to transfer my school to the town of Corbeil, which is nearer to the city of Paris, so that there opportunity might furnish more frequent contests of disputation."

Not long after this, however, Abelard was "stricken with an infirmity," which he claimed was brought about by overstudy. He was obliged to return to his home in Brittany where he apparently remained for a number of years.

His family, especially his mother, Lucie, welcomed him. But after his experiences in the wider world of Paris and its intellectual climate, Abelard was restless and bored during his long convalescence. He had no intention of quitting the career he had embarked upon, and he used the months of enforced leisure to study and to cultivate his own theories and philosophy. He had no interest in helping his father and brothers protect and run their estate, nor did he get much pleasure from the social activities around him. If there were pretty young women who set their caps for him, Abelard managed to ignore them. The absorbing passion of his life, up to then, was the gathering of knowledge. It left him no time for the lighter pleasures of love and war.

During his absence, William of Champeaux was made bishop of Chalons, where he opened another school. When the news of this reached Abelard, he recovered at once from his infirmity. With the sublime impudence that was so characteristic of him, he returned to William's classes, ostensibly to learn rhetoric. But once again he contrived to challenge his old master's authority by beating him in argument and forcing the older man to alter his statements.

When Abelard was ordered out of his classes by the enraged William, who by now had become an enemy, he opened his own school again at Melun and drew most of William's students with him.

In his own words, "Then I, returning to Melun, established my school there as before. And the more openly his jealousy pursued me the more widely it increased my authority, according to the words of the poet: 'Envy seeketh the heights, the winds blow on the mountaintops.'"

When William was forced to abandon his school at Chalons, Abelard made an attempt to step into his place, but he found that another master had already been appointed. So Abelard "pitched the tent" of his own school on Mount Ste. Genevieve, just outside of Paris—as though in defiance of the substitute master William had dared to appoint.

"'Shouldst thou demand the issue of this fight,'" Abelard wrote, quoting Ajax, "'I was not vanquished by mine enemy.'"

There can be no doubt that Abelard was enjoying himself in

this battle with William of Champeaux, ill-advised as it may have been. Although he never forgot that his real quest was for truth, he didn't mind tilting at a few windmills on his way or cracking a few swollen heads in the process. That his methods were enjoyed by the students is proven by the fact that, of the five thousand or more who came to Paris to study, at least three thousand gathered wherever Abelard taught, in preference to the other masters.

For all his faults of pride, impudence, and lack of respect for so-called authority, Abelard was one of the pioneers in the new movement of the Middle Ages toward learning for learning's sake. He had a genuine vocation for scholarship, as others had for religion. Peter the Venerable, the famous abbot of Cluny, called him the proudest scholar in Europe. He was also called one of the "makers of life"—one of the most important in twelfth-century Europe.

At this point in his career, however, there was another interruption. This time it was an urgent message from his mother, asking him to return home. When he arrived at Pallet after an anxious journey, he found that his father had decided to become a monk, and that his "dearest mother" was about to follow her husband's example and take the veil.

In his own detailed recital of the woes that befell him, Abelard gave little more than a few sentences to this event. And yet it must have come as a shock to him as it was to his brothers and sister.

What Berenger and Lucie were contemplating, however, was not so drastic or unusual a step as it would be today. The religious fervor of the Middle Ages, and the growth of the monasteries and convents, had influenced many other married and prosperous men and women to seek the religious and contemplative life. Berenger had sons who would carry on the business of his estate. Denise, the daughter, was married and mature enough to look after domestic matters. Berenger and Lucie, looking forward to an idle old age, had decided to give their remaining years to the service of God.

Abelard, in spite of relinquishing the rights of an older son, had shown on many occasions a depth of warm feeling toward his family. It moved him that they had sent for him in this moment of great decision. There is proof of his concern in the fact that he abruptly abandoned his successful school, risking the loss of his students to jealous masters. This would have meant the loss not only of his only means of livelihood but of the adulation that was more important to him than food or drink.

In spite of this danger to his career, Abelard remained in Brittany for some months, until he had seen both parents depart with encouragement from their children instead of reproach. Then, after advising his brothers and consoling his sister, Abelard left home once more.

But now, having been influenced, no doubt, by his parents' example, Abelard decided to take up the serious study of theology. He chose for his instructor William of Champeaux's own master, Anselm of Laon. Of him, Abelard wrote as follows: "I came therefore to this old man, who owed his name rather to long familiarity than to his intelligence or his memory. To whom if anyone came knocking at his door in uncertainty as to some question, he departed more uncertain still. . . . His fluency of words was admirable, but in sense they were contemptible and devoid of reason. When he kindled a fire he filled his house with smoke, rather than lighted it with a blaze. His tree, in full life, was conspicuous from afar, but by those who stood near and diligently examined the same, it was found to be barren."

After he had attended Anselm's classes for a few weeks, Abelard showed up for lectures more and more rarely. For this he was criticized by some of the old teacher's more devoted disciples as showing contempt for so important a master. Abelard shrugged his shoulders and let them know he considered them misguided apes.

One day, as a class was breaking up, a certain student asked Abelard what he thought about the reading of the Holy Scriptures. Having up to then devoted himself almost exclusively to a study of the sciences, Abelard replied that he thought such reading could be most salutary, since it was the lore in which the salvation of the soul is revealed. However, he couldn't resist adding that he marveled that to literate men the scriptures should not be sufficient, so that they should require no other instruction regarding them.

Many of those present laughed at Abelard, and asked if he could presume to explain what he had read. Quick to accept a challenge, Abelard answered that he was ready to try it if they wished. Whereupon, after consulting among themselves, they brought him the most obscure passages of *Ezekiel*, and asked him to interpret them.

The next day Abelard invited them all to a lecture on *Ezekiel*. Astonished, the students undertook to give him good advice, saying that he should by no means make haste, but devote himself, instead, for a much longer time to the preparation of his interpretation, so that he should offset his inexperience by hard and diligent work.

To this Abelard replied indignantly that it was not his custom to achieve success by plodding routine but by his ability. He added that he would abandon the project altogether unless they would agree to attend his lecture that very day.

"In truth," Abelard wrote, "at this first lecture of mine only a few were present, for it seemed quite absurd to all of them that I, hitherto so inexperienced in discussing the scriptures, should attempt the thing so hastily. However, this lecture gave such satisfaction to all those who heard it that they spread its praises abroad with enthusiasm, and thus compelled me to continue my interpretation of the sacred text.

"When word of this was noised about, those who had stayed away from the first lecture came eagerly, some to the second, and more to the third, and all of them were eager to write down the glosses which I had begun on the first day, so as to have them all from the very beginning."

As an example of Abelard's supreme self-confidence, not to say arrogance, this passage from his *Historia Calamitatum* is most illuminating. It is also an example of his personal charm and ability to win over even a hostile audience. For those who came to jeer so often remained to applaud. It was the kind of success that the youthful Abelard enjoyed the most, just as he enjoyed pulling the props from under the most respected teachers of his day.

It may be that all this was due to the exuberance of youth, since Abelard never showed any streak of actual cruelty in his nature, either in the days when his star was high or when adversity overtook him. He did possess one of the keenest minds of his generation, and he was always several steps ahead of everyone else in his thinking. He could not easily suffer fools or charlatans, much less allow them to come between him and his eager search for the truth.

Certainly there is no reason to ascribe his arrogance, in terms of modern psychiatry, to an inferiority complex or sense of insecurity, whether deep-seated or not. Abelard was wellborn, he had no serious financial problems, he had led a happy childhood. And, up to this time, he had succeeded in everything he set his heart and mind on doing. He was exceptionally handsome, virile, and well able to defend himself physically and mentally. If he tended to parade his superiority over smaller minds and souls, it could have been that this was the way he most enjoyed himself.

At any rate, he showed and felt no pity for the venerable Anselm, who was soon acutely smitten with envy and annoyed by the impressions Abelard was making on his own students. Egged on by others whom Abelard had annoyed in one way or other, Anselm began to persecute Abelard for lecturing on the scriptures no less bitterly than William of Champeaux had done for his work in philosophy.

There were two scholars in Anselm's school at that time, who were said to excel the others. These two were Alberic of Rheims and Lotulphe, the Lombard. Having exalted opinions of themselves, as Abelard pointed out, they became incensed at the newcomer and persuaded the old man to forbid Abelard to carry on any further the work of preparing glosses for the students in his school.

Anselm's excuse was that if, by chance, any blunders should appear in this work—which he considered likely enough in view of Abelard's lack of training—the errors would be attributed to him.

The unfairness of this, filled the students with indignation, but there was nothing they could do. And so Abelard, denied a lecture platform at Laon, left there and returned to Paris. There he was now permitted to direct the school from which he had once been driven out by William of Champeaux.

He completed the glosses he had begun on *Ezekiel*, and these were so well received that Abelard was asked to lecture on theology as well as philosophy. This was indeed success.

Abelard's fame was now at its height. He was liked as well as admired, not only by his students but by any of the populace of the city with whom he had contact. Those songs that he had composed in idle moments, for his own amusement, were now on everyone's lips. Lovers as well as pedants had only words of praise for Abelard. His cup was running over!

But then, as he himself wrote of this peak in his career:

"Prosperity always puffs up the foolish, and wordly comfort enervates the soul, rendering it an easy prey to carnal temptations.

"Thus I, who by this time had come to regard myself as the only philosopher remaining in the whole world, and had ceased to fear any further disturbance to my peace, began to loosen the reins of my desires, although hitherto I had always lived in the utmost continence."

"O nightingale, give over
For an hour,
Till the heart sings. . . ."

4

This fragment of a poem would have been written, Helen Waddell claims in *The Wandering Scholars*, ". . . even if Abelard had not come to neglect the schools for a windflower of seventeen growing in the shadow of Notre Dame, and set her lovely name to melodies lovelier still."

If Heloise had mingled with the students in the cloisters of Notre Dame where Abelard held his classes, he had singled her out and been aware of her before he carefully arranged for their meeting. It is certain he had heard of her, this brilliant girl who could converse in Latin with as much ease as he, and whose learning was equal to, if it did not indeed surpass, that of his brightest student.

As he lectured on the universals or on the early Hebrew prophets, he noticed that eager, beautiful face turned up to him; the large, inquiring gray eyes, the slender form in its long, dove-gray tunic. Her rapt attention flattered him, who thirsted so for adulation, and he felt, reasonably enough, that here was fertile soil indeed, not only for the seeds of his own wisdom but for love.

In spite of his continence thus far, he may have been stirred to a physical response by the appearance of a young girl there in a crowd of boys. He speaks of loosening the reins of his desire at that very time. Had it already happened, and did Heloise, by her presence among his students, become merely the chance object of those already loosened desires? It is difficult to say, because Abelard's account of their first meeting was written by him many years later, when, by circumstance rather than age, the biological urge was gone.

Abelard was no longer a youth, however, when desire first overcame his scruples, or whatever it was that had kept him chaste. Until then, he seems to have had no time for the joys that the poets described and of which the minstrels sang. With his wish to be first in everything, and with his pride in conquest, it is strange that he had not yet stooped to what would have been for him the easiest conquest of all—that of women.

Now, suddenly, by his own admission he found himself ripe for love or, as he chose to regard it when he wrote the following passage so long afterward, lust.

"Since, therefore," he wrote in the *Historia Calamitatum*, "I ever abhorred the uncleanness of harlots, and was withheld from the society of noblewomen by the assiduity of my studies, nor had ever held much conversation with those of the common sort, lewd fortune, as the saying is, caressing me, found a more convenient opportunity whereby she might the more easily dash me down from the pinnacle of sublimity; so that in my overweening pride, and unmindful of the grace I had received, divine pity might recall me humbled to itself."

Abelard had no difficulty arranging for a meeting with Heloise. He already knew Canon Fulbert, and it was simple enough to secure an invitation to visit the house on the Rue des Chantres.

Fulbert was somewhat of an intellectual snob, and he was honored by a visit from Abelard, the foremost scholar of his day. He put himself out to be a gracious host, displaying the greatest treasures in his library—as well as his niece, of whom he was by now almost as proud.

Abelard, his mind filled with but a single idea, admired the library, and then, as if to compliment his host, expressed his envy of the canon, who lived so comfortably, with a servant to care for his wants, whereas he, Abelard, had to be content with mere lodgings.

Heloise, learning the name of her uncle's guest, made an appearance. She wore her most becoming tunic, and allotted

more time than usual to her toilette. And it was with quite understandable pride that Fulbert presented his niece to his distinguished visitor.

While Fulbert poured more wine into the goblets and talked
in the garrulous manner of an old man, there was plenty of
opportunity for Abelard and Heloise to study each other and
even to make known by a glance or a smile, the extent to which
each was impressed.

How long did it take before Abelard boldly made the propo-
sition that was to change the lives of them all irrevocably? His
suggestion, when it came, was that he be allowed to rent the
little spare room upstairs, for which privilege Abelard would, in
addition to paying a modest sum of money, undertake to instruct
the canon's niece in subjects of which she was still ignorant.

Fulbert was said to have been avaricious, but, to do him
justice, he was also anxious that his niece should have every
possible opportunity to increase her already phenomenal fund
of knowledge. It was, therefore, for both these reasons that he
eagerly accepted Abelard's proposal and rented him the small
room in his house. But still another reason was that he knew
he would be the envy of all his colleagues for having so distinguished a scholar under his roof, and that thereby he would
gather in his modest parlor the finest minds in Europe. Who
knew but that the prestige this would bring him might advance
his career as a cleric? Fulbert considered the arrangement a piece
of sheer good luck, and was in the best of humors.

Not long after this first meeting, therefore, Abelard and
Heloise found themselves living in the same house, with no
obstacle in the way of their mutual and almost spontaneous desire other than a rather deaf and shortsighted old man who, for
all his scholarship, could not have been very wise.

The higher education of Heloise began almost at once, or as
soon as Abelard moved in. The canon, still considering his niece
a child, cautioned the famous teacher to be strict with her and,
if she showed any reluctance to study, to punish her as he would
any reluctant student in his classes.

"Whereupon earnestly beseeching me," Abelard wrote, "he

acceeded to my wishes farther than I had presumed to hope, and served the purpose of my love: committing her wholly to my mastership, that as often as I returned from my school, whether by day or by night, if I had the time, I was to instruct her. And, if I found her idle, he gave me permission to chastise her. In which matter I was no less amazed, while marveling at his simplicity, than if he had entrusted a tender lamb to a ravening wolf. . . ."

In fairness to Fulbert, one must remember, first, his love for his niece, and second, the reputation of Abelard for his past continence. These were enough to keep him from having any base suspicions.

"In face she was not inferior to other women," Abelard wrote, which would have been faint praise indeed, had it not been written when any thought of the beauty of women was forbidden.

But he goes on: "In the abundance of learning she was supreme. For inasmuch as this advantage, namely literary knowledge, is rare in women, so did it more commend the girl. . . . Seeing in her, therefore, all those things that are wont to attract lovers, I thought it suitable to join her to myself in love and believed that I could effect this most easily."

However Abelard tried to explain the origin of that flame which was to consume them both, as he wrote of it in those later years when his heart was cold to emotions, the truth remains that this was no ordinary seduction. It was a spontaneous and mutual love, voluntarily offered and received. Heloise, showing no reticence whatever, always insisted on accepting her own responsibility for the consequences.

Abelard, still youthful and handsome, although some twenty years older than Heloise, had no reason to expect a refusal from any woman to whom he made advances. However, it never seemed to have occurred to him that some women might be attracted by the quality of his mind, the courageousness of his spirit, and, not least, the glamor of his fame, as well as his masculine beauty. The combination was irresistible to a young intellectual such as Heloise.

There is no record to tell of what those first lessons consisted. Heloise's learning was deep, but there were many things she had not learned. Perhaps among these was the correct way to read Latin verse. Abelard, the poet, had much to teach her in the matter of rhythm and meter.

Taking up a volume of the canon's precious *Aeneid,* he cautioned her to feel the meter of a poem as if it were a hymn sung in church. "Do not scan," he said, correcting her reading, "but read continuously, feeling the words and the sense and observing the main divisions with an almost imperceptible but conscious pause."

And then, in his beautiful voice, he read aloud the beginning of Vergil's epic: "*Arma virumque cano, Troiae qui primus . . .*" until the book slipped from his fingers to the table, and he reached to take the small hand of Heloise into his own. It was only natural that, after looking into those eager, worshiping, gray eyes, he should put his lips upon hers, as if to seal one lesson, only to begin another—one about which she knew far less than she did of the scanning of Latin verse.

In the long hours of the night, when the house was silent and Fulbert was asleep downstairs by the fire that, though carefully banked, gave still a little comfort to old bones, no one heard the soft footsteps of the lovers as they mounted the stairs to the bedroom of Heloise, or the whispers that were as caressing as the sound of doves.

There is no question that Abelard deliberately set out to seduce the young girl who had been placed in his charge by her uncle. It was then, and will always remain in the eyes of the world a contemptible act. And yet Heloise never regarded her surrender as a seduction, nor did she ever reproach her lover for it.

From the moment she saw Abelard, and even before that, perhaps, when she had merely heard tales about the master and longed to meet him, Heloise was in love. Not by any gesture or word would she have repulsed the overtures made by one whom she already adored—not even if she had realized how quickly they would lead to graver sins. In fact there is no evidence that she regarded her surrender or her lover's deed as a sin at all.

Abelard was later to recall with disgust and loathing his part in this act, which he called lust. But, to Heloise, their desire for each other and the gratification of that desire, were the natural expressions of love. Her surrender was complete, not only of her body and of that state of virginity upon which men set so great a value, but of her heart and mind and soul. Love was of enough grandeur to transcend lust. What was more, to Heloise it had the power to wash human sins and turn them white as snow.

There can be no doubt, on the other hand, that Abelard was well aware at the time that he was committing a twofold sin: against the virgin who had been entrusted to him, and against the old man who was proud to consider him a colleague and a friend, a man whose hospitality he was now so basely abusing.

However, if Abelard began the seduction of Heloise lightly, it was not long before he was as deeply involved as she. They were bound to each other by something much stronger than the human will. He could not now, with a belated show of conscience, withdraw. The trap had been sprung, and they were both inextricably caught in it—for life.

And yet, as if to excuse himself, as well as to put the blame to some extent on Fulbert, Abelard wrote:

"For in giving her to me, not only to be taught but to be vehemently chastised, what else was he doing than giving every license to my desires and providing an opportunity whereby, even if I did not wish, if I could not move her by blandishments I might the more easily bend her by threats and blows. . . . What more need I say? First in one house we were united, then in one mind. So, under the pretext of discipline, we abandoned ourselves utterly to love, and those secret retreats which love demands, the study of our texts afforded us.

"And so, our books lying open between us, more words of love rose to our lips than of literature, kisses were more frequent than speech. Oftener went our hands to each other's bosom than to the pages; love turned our eyes more frequently to itself than it directed them to the study of the texts. That we might be less suspected, blows were given at times, by love, not anger, affection not indignation, which surpassed all ointments in their sweetness."

And so, according to Abelard, "No stage of love was omitted . . . and if love could elaborate anything new, that we took in addition."

The less experienced they both were, the more they experimented, and the less satiety did they find in their love-making. The labyrinthine ways of sexual expression were as fresh and new to Abelard as they were to Heloise. The world of sensuality was one they entered together, by the same gate. The fire that Abelard had started engulfed them both. The longer it burned, the more impossible it was to extinguish—since it was fed by its own flames.

It was inevitable that this new preoccupation should have caused Abelard to neglect his school and the teaching of philosophy. He found his classes tedious and teaching laborious. Not only that, it was impossible for him to keep awake during the daytime because of the nights he was spending with Heloise. Bored with the subjects that had once delighted him and kept his students spellbound, he now gave his lectures in so negligent and lethargic a fashion that no one got anything out of them. He himself said of this period that he produced nothing new from his own mind but only from memory, and therefore was nothing but a "reciter of things learned in the past."

Instead of preparing new lectures, he found time now only to compose verses of an amorous nature. These were copied and passed from hand to hand, and were soon being sung all over France. And since he mentioned his beloved by name, others began writing verses about the fair Heloise, some of which were extremely audacious, even pornographic. The students were well aware, by this time, of the cause of their master's preoccupation, and why his lectures were so dull. Like students of all times, they could not resist making up jokes at their master's expense.

The gossip and the poems, though bordering on the obscene, were not malicious, however. Codes of morals, as we well know, change with the centuries. During the lifetime of Heloise and

Abelard their romance brought them no discredit in the public eye, nor did it in the ages immediately following. It has been said that it was the Puritans, much later, who placed sexual sin at the head of the list. During the Middle Ages, it would seem that the sins of pride, envy, malicious gossip, and anger were considered more deadly.

As Ralph Adams Cram explained in his introduction to a comparatively new translation of the *Historia Calamitatum*, "The twelfth and thirteenth centuries were not an age of moral laxity: ideals and standards and conduct were immeasurably higher than they had been for five hundred years, higher than they were to be in the centuries that followed the crest of the Middle Ages. It was, however, a time of enormous vitality, of throbbing energy that was constantly bursting its bounds, as well as a time of personal liberty and freedom of action that would seem strange to us in these days of endless legal restraint and inhibitions."

It would seem, from her letters, that Heloise, far from regarding her love affair as something shameful that was to be hidden, took pride in the knowledge that she was now spoken of as Abelard's mistress. Was she not envied by all the great ladies who heard Abelard's songs and knew of his fame and had even seen him and admired his beauty? What knights of theirs, in all their courts of love, could compare with her beloved? Who would not be proud to be the mistress of so great a man? How fortunate she was, an orphan with nothing to offer but her mind and her young person, to have been chosen, from among all those titled and lovely ladies, to be called Abelard's own love!

Except when the world intruded itself upon them, Heloise and Abelard were absorbed in each other. "The same trance," Helen Waddell wrote in her *Wandering Scholars*, "fell on the quiet house in the Rue des Chantres as on a ship becalmed off the Cornish coast: and the two drank together a cup as fatal as the love draught of Tristan and Isolde."

Abelard had many gifts to win a woman's heart, but the one that was rarest in a scholar and a philosopher was his ability to write songs both in the classic meter and in the new style of rhyming that was coming into vogue, and of setting them to music so lovely that even the illiterate could sing them.

It is a pity that none of Abelard's songs for Heloise have come down to us complete. There are a few fragments attributed to him, such as the "Hours," he is supposed to have written for her when, as Helen Waddell said, "the sword lay between them." Among the poems are a half dozen laments of Dinah for her ruined lover, one for the daughter of Jephthah dead in her virginity, and a poem about David and Jonathan. And some doubt has been cast upon the authenticity of these, although the meters are exquisite and are typical of Abelard's style, and the subject matter is poignant enough to have been written when the passion between Heloise and Abelard was about to be discovered by her uncle, and crucified.

> Low in thy grave with thee
>   Happy to lie,
> Since there's no greater thing left Love to do.
>   And to live after thee
>   Is but to die,
> For with but half a soul what can Life do?
>
>   So share thy victory
>   Or else thy grave,
> Either to rescue thee, or with thee lie;
>   Ending that life for thee,
>   That thou didst save,
> So Death, that sundereth, might bring more nigh.
>
>   Peace, O my stricken Lute!
>   Thy strings are sleeping.
>   Would that my heart could still
>   Its bitter weeping.

The love story of Heloise and Abelard has been told by other poets: in the twelfth century's *Metamorphosis*, and at the end of the thirteenth century, by Jean de Meung, the young clerk who first translated the *Letters*. By the fifteenth century, Francois Villon had included Heloise among the "*dames du temps jadis*."

> *Où est la tres sage Hellois,*
> *Pour qui fut chastré et puis moyne*
> *Pierre Esbaillart à Saint-Denis?*
> *Pour son amour ot cest essoyne. . . .*
> *Mais où sont les neiges d'antan!*

And as late as the first half of the eighteenth century, Alexander Pope wrote "Eloisa to Abelard," in which poem are the lines: "Love the offender, yet detest the offence," and "Curse on all laws but those which love has made!"

Abelard may have destroyed his own songs during those bitter years when he repented that which had brought him his greatest happiness and his most cruel misery. But Helen Waddell has said that it is hardly possible that the songs of so famous a singer should have perished altogether. Here and there, she thinks, a lyric can be found that has caught something of the "shattering ecstasy of their fire" and may be Abelard's. It may be even so delicate a lyric as this, that slipped into the thirteenth-century *Romance of the Rose.*

> Take thou this rose, O rose,
> Since love's own flower it is.
> And by that rose
> Thy lover captive is.

5

Canon Fulbert seems to have been the last person to discover what was going on in his own house. Even if some of the gossip reached his ears, he brushed it aside, unable to believe anything so base of the two he loved—Abelard, whom he trusted, and his niece, Heloise, whom he still thought of as a child.

As Abelard wrote, "For not readily do we suspect baseness in those whom we most love . . . whence comes the saying of St. Jerome in his Epistle to Sabinian, 'We are always the last to learn of the evils of our own house, and remain ignorant of the vices of our children and wives when they are a song among the neighbors. But what one is the last to know, one does at any rate come to know in time, and what all have learned is not easy to keep hidden from one.'"

And so it was that several months went by before Fulbert's eyes were opened to what was going on under his roof. We are never told exactly when he made the discovery, or how. All we know is that he immediately ordered Abelard from the house.

Abelard's account describes only the emotions of the lovers at this separation, and not the uncle's anguish when the truth was made known to him.

"What was their grief at their parting!" Abelard exclaims. "What blushing and confusion for me! With what contrition . . . was I afflicted! What floods of tears had she to bear at my shame! Yet, neither complained of what had befallen himself, but each for the other's misfortune."

One cannot help feeling sorrier, at this point, for Canon Fulbert than for the lovers. It isn't easy to be faced with the results of one's own folly. Certainly he had lived in the world long enough to realize that he had handed over his niece to her seducer in a way that was, however generous and trusting, almost criminally shortsighted.

Heloise had been placed in his care first as an infant and then as a young girl by the nuns of the convent of Argenteuil, who had reared her carefully. He had come to love her, else why would he have kept her with him for two precious years? He was proud of her, obviously, or he would not have seized the opportunity to obtain for her the best teacher in all of France.

But he should not have let himself be blinded to the fact that Abelard, in spite of his reputation for celibacy, was adored everywhere he went, by women as well as men; that he was not only a brilliant scholar and teacher, but a handsome and vigorous man with a tremendous amount of charm and personal magnetism.

And Heloise was not only a precocious student, she was a lovely young girl at a most susceptible age. Because she was intellectual did not mean that she was not highly romantic and capable of deep passions once they were aroused. Anyone with the slightest perception could have seen, as the nuns at Argenteuil had seen, that beneath that quiet surface was a smoldering fire waiting for the touch that would cause it to burst into flame.

It did not help Fulbert to recover from the shock of his betrayal to realize that he had brought on the situation himself by his own fatuity and blindness. Indeed it is quite possible that this was one of the factors responsible for the extreme, almost insane, measure he later took to avenge himself.

There was a debasing scene when Fulbert made his discovery. One can imagine the flood of tears, though it is hard to think of Abelard blushing. They must have known they would be discovered someday, and yet, when has the fear of discovery ever stopped two people caught up in a consuming passion?

Abelard expressed his concern for the plight of the young girl, for which he was to blame. Yet was he not as much concerned for the figure he made in his own world? It is easy to understand how humiliating it was for so proud a man to read, in the faces of a once admiring body of colleagues and students, something that could be interpreted as pity, censure, or—even worse— amusement.

Heloise, on the other hand, was not so concerned with herself as with Abelard and the effect the disclosure would have on him and his future. There was never, from the very beginning, an iota of selfishness in the love of Heloise for Abelard. It was not easy to continue to live in the same house with her outraged uncle, to hear his reproaches, to face his scorn, to be forced to listen to tirades of abuse heaped on her absent lover. But what was far worse was the belief that, because of her, any misfortune might come to the man she adored.

As for Abelard, he wrote only that the separation from each other physically meant that they were drawn closer by the "coupling" of their minds, and that the denial of satisfaction served to inflame their love still further. . . .

Not long after their secret was discovered and Abelard had been ordered to leave the house on the Rue des Chantres, Heloise found that she was pregnant. A prisoner in her uncle's home, where once she had been cherished as a daughter, there was no one in whom she could confide, no other woman to whom she could turn for advice.

While Heloise was still a pupil in the convent of Argenteuil, she had noticed certain changes in the appearance of a peasant girl who came from the village regularly to assist the nuns at their menial chores. Later this same girl gave birth to a child. The incident then seemed to have no more significance than the yearly birth of little lambs and calves at Argenteuil. The nuns found a home for the baby and kept the girl on to work for them as before. But now, as Heloise recalled the incident, the peasant girl's travail had been merely an animal process, a part of the workings of nature in the spring of the year. What was happening to herself was something different—because it was

the result of love. The fruit of the passion she had shared with
Abelard must have something of the divine, the miraculous,
about it. There was no comparison between this and the earth-
born infant of the young peasant girl. Her love and Abelard's
had been noble, and this product of it, this child she would
produce, would be ennobled by it.

And so, quieting the fears that would have been more natural
under the circumstances, Heloise rejoiced. She managed to send
a message to Abelard, telling him of their child that she was
carrying close to her heart, and asking him to decide what was
to be done. She was afraid only of what might happen when
her uncle discovered the fact, which he soon must do.

Abelard, revealing his essential decency and the depth of his
love, assumed full responsibility for and control of the situation.
He made arrangements at once to remove Heloise and his un-
born child to a place of safety.

". . . And so, on a certain night," Abelard wrote, "her uncle
being absent, as we had planned, I took her by stealth from his
house and carried her to my own country without delay. Where,
in my sister's house she stayed until such time as she was delivered of a son whom she named Astrolabe."

Those months of peace and quiet in Abelard's own country,
Brittany, where she was tenderly cared for by his devoted sister,
who welcomed her because Abelard loved her and also for herself, were among the few happy times Heloise had known or
would ever know.

She had never experienced what it was like to live in the
heart of a large family. Her earliest memories of life with her
own mother were dim, if she retained any at all. All that she
really remembered were the years as an orphan at the convent
of Argenteuil, and the two years she had spent in the bachelor
establishment of her uncle.

The large house at Pallet, with its slate turrets and window
frames; the busy kitchen hung with hams and dried herbs and
glistening copper pots; the children tumbling about and getting
underfoot; the farmyard noises and activities; the fields and the
woods that one could roam in at will; the streams with speckled

trout—above all, the atmosphere of health and good nature, affection and mutual respect—delighted Heloise. And it was especially precious to her since all of it was part of the youth of the man she loved.

What was even more gratifying was the fact that, whereas everyone she had known admired Abelard and treated him with respect, even awe, these people among whom she now dwelt loved him as she loved him, as a human being, a creature of flesh and blood. He was their elder brother—and her beloved. She and his sister, Denise, had their love for Abelard in common, and it made a bond between them such as Heloise had never had with anyone, not with the mother superior or the nuns who were her teachers at Argenteuil, and certainly not with her uncle. She had found a real family at last, and, while she was bearing Abelard's child, she was as happy as she could possibly be without his presence too.

Her happiness would have been complete had Abelard been able to remain with her. But he had been forced to conduct his classes in Paris. Had he left them for any length of time, so soon after the event about which there had been been so much scandal, it would have been difficult for him to establish himself again as a master. But Heloise knew he would be coming to see her as soon as the talk died down, and that then they would be together openly, and no longer have to hide their love for each other as if it were a shameful thing, instead of the glory she felt it to be.

Things were not easy now for Abelard. He was only too aware, as he stood before his students in the cloister of Notre Dame, that their sympathies, as well as those of the canons, were with Fulbert, who had been crying out his wrongs to the world.

Abelard, in his account of his calamities, wrote that Fulbert, after the flight of Heloise, was ". . . almost driven mad. With what grief he boiled, with what shame he was overwhelmed, no one who had not beheld him could imagine. How he should act towards me, what snares he should lay for me he knew not. If he were to kill me, or injure my body in any way, he feared greatly lest his beloved niece might be made to pay the penalty in my country. To seize my person and coerce me anywhere against my will was of no avail, seeing that I was constantly on my guard in this respect, because I had no doubt that he would speedily assault me if it were worth his while or if he dared."

Abelard, after his abrupt expulsion from the canon's house, found lodgings in the Latin Quarter (so called because the students who lived there spoke to each other in Latin rather than in their own tongues, to practice and perhaps display their learning). On his way to and from the Petit Pont, which he had to cross, there was no way to avoid passing close by the house on the Rue des Chantres—with the daily risk of encountering Fulbert.

For a man as proud as Abelard, the idea of making detours to avoid a scene was intolerable. There was only one thing to do, he decided, and that was to meet Fulbert on his own ground, and to try to affect a reconciliation, by whatever means or compromise possible, in order to "save face"—not only his own, but Fulbert's.

"At length," Abelard wrote, "I, in some compassion for his exceeding anxiety, and vehemently accusing myself of the fraud which my love had forced me to commit, as if it were the basest treachery, went to supplicate the man, promising also such amends as he himself would prescribe. Nor, I asserted, did what I had committed appear remarkable to any who had experienced the force of love, or who could remember the ruin to which even the greatest men, from the very beginning of the human race, had been brought down by women."

Whether this attitude, which was hardly fair to Heloise, did anything to console the outraged canon or not, Abelard was prepared to go even further. "And that I might conciliate him beyond all that he could hope," Abelard wrote, "I offered him the satisfaction of joining her whom I had corrupted to myself in marriage, provided that this were done in secret lest I incurred any detriment to my reputation. He assented, and with his own word and a kiss, as well as with those of his household, sealed the concord that I had required of him, the more easily to betray me."

The interview seemed to be a successful one. No blood was shed, although Abelard had every reason to fear for his safety. A bargain was sealed—but only after Fulbert had promised that the marriage would be kept secret. And yet, would it not have required the most extreme arrogance, pride, or self-love, to believe in such a promise from a grief-crazed old man? Heloise knew better!

When Abelard mentioned the danger to his career that news of his marriage might incur, he was not exaggerating. As a teacher of philosophy and theology, he was a clerk rather than an ecclesiastic, and, having never taken orders, he could marry. But this would have been contrary to custom in the twelfth century. Most teachers connected with the universities abstained from marriage in order to be free to carry on their studies and to move from place to place as it seemed necessary. To have a wife and family trailing after him, would not only have been inconvenient but undignified.

Furthermore, marriage barred a clerk from the ecclesiastical preferment which so famous a teacher as Abelard had every reason to expect. It was for this reason that he obtained a promise from Fulbert to keep the marriage a secret.

And yet, in spite of the danger to his career and the jeopardizing of his brilliant future, Abelard offered to marry Heloise. It was proof enough that, in spite of his high regard for himself and his mission in the world of letters, Abelard loved her, and pitied the uncle whom he had wronged. His character was as full of contradictions as that of most men, and the more fascinating because of it. But it is why Abelard never quite attains the noble stature of Heloise, and why, unlike his archenemy, Bernard, who came into the picture later, he never even aspired to being called a saint.

6

Abelard wrote: "Straightway returning to my country, I brought back my mistress that I might make her my wife. She, however, did not at all approve this action, nay, utterly deprecated it for two reasons, namely the danger as well as the disgrace to myself."

It may be hard for any of us unfamiliar with the medieval mind to understand why Heloise should have tried so passionately to discourage her lover from doing what would seem the most honorable thing. Marriage, we would think, would clear her name and, what was more important, it would legalize her son.

But it is necessary to remember that Heloise, in spite of the qualities we recognize and admire in her today, was entirely a product and member of twelfth-century society. Marriage, even for a woman, was not looked upon then as it is today. Henry Osborn Taylor, in *The Medieval Mind*, has said that marriage was, of course, holy in the name of Christ, but, during the centuries that saw the rise of monasticism and priestly celibacy, the world was shown a way of life holier and purer than that bestowed by the marriage sacrament, a way that demanded the ideal best of every man and woman. It could not help but cast a reflection on whatever fell below such high standards. The medieval church, emphasizing as it did the virgin or celibate state, gave the world a higher ideal than marriage to admire and imitate.

Heloise was imbued with this viewpoint. She felt that in Abelard's case, marriage would only serve to stress the sin he had already committed, his fall from the prescribed state of celibacy. As for herself, she felt that her sin was relatively unimportant. In fact, she regarded herself as in no way disgraced for having loved Abelard and borne him a son.

So deep was her love for Abelard that, under any social system, she would have sacrificed herself for him. But brought up as she was, and reflecting her own period as she did, Heloise could only feel that marriage, without changing their personal relationship, would make her the unwilling cause of Abelard's downfall, and would lead to the abandonment of his vocation.

As for the argument that by marrying Abelard she would be giving her son a great and proud name, instead of the stigma of bastard, it must also be recalled that in the twelfth century it was no disgrace to be a bastard. That was to come later, as civilization advanced.

For several days and nights there in Brittany, Heloise argued with her lover against their marriage. Perhaps never has any woman made so passionate and, at the same time, so coldly intellectual a plea against a ritual that was devised for her benefit and her protection.

She dwelt first on the danger and the disgrace their marriage would bring to Abelard. She was certain that her uncle would never be satisfied with this appeasement, a marriage that was to be kept a secret. (In this she was proved to be right.) She demanded to know what glory she could have in her husband, if she should first make him inglorious. What penalties would the world demand of her if she should rob it of so shining a light? What condemnation would follow such a loss to the church—what laments among philosophers! How regrettable it would be for him, whom nature had made for the whole world, to devote himself to one woman alone!

Turning to more homely arguments, Heloise demanded that Abelard consider the conditions of honorable wedlock. She asked what possible accord there could be between scholars and domestic servants, between books and distaffs, between the pen

and the spindle. What man, intent on his religious or philosophical meditations, could possibly endure the whining of
children, the lullabies of a nurse trying to soothe them, or the
noisy confusion, on the whole, of domestic life?

The rich, she conceded, might manage to combine study and
domesticity, but they lived in palaces with many rooms and
could get away from the squalor and the tumult. Their very
wealth protected them from daily worries and annoyances. It
was different with poor scholars and philosophers, who could
not be expected to fill their minds with worldly cares and yet
have time for religious and philosophical study.

She quoted passages from the New Testament in which the
disciples were exhorted never to marry. She invoked St. Jerome,
who, in his first book against Jovinianus, set forth in great detail
the intolerable annoyances and the endless disturbances of
married life, proving that no wise man would voluntarily choose
such a state. She also reminded Abelard that Cicero, on being
asked to marry the sister of Hircius, replied that he would not,
since he could not give his attention at the same time to a wife
and to philosophy.

She quoted Seneca, who said that philosophy was not a thing
to be studied only in hours of leisure. One must give up everything else in order to devote oneself to it, for no amount of time
is actually enough.

It matters little, she pointed out, whether one gives up the
study of philosophy entirely, or only interrupts it, because a
thought can never remain at the point where it was when the
interruption comes. Therefore, she said, it is impossible to adjust
life to include domesticity and philosophy. If Abelard were to
continue his studies and his teaching, everything else must be
eliminated.

Was this so impossible? Was it not true that in every race
there have always been a few who excelled the rest because of
the purity of their lives and their devotion to God—or to philosophy and wisdom. These were set apart from the multitude
by their continence and their abstinence from worldly pleasures.

As examples, she gave the Nazarites, the Sadducees, and the Essenes. Were there not teachers even now, she asked, who kept themselves apart from the multitude that they might be the more worthy to teach the great truths they discovered?

"If you scorn the reverence due to God," Heloise said to Abelard in this most amazing of arguments, "let regard for your reputation temper your shamelessness. Remember that Socrates was chained to a wife, and by what filthy accident he paid for this blot on philosophy! If you care nothing for your privileges as a cleric, at least uphold your dignity as a philosopher."

Whether Abelard was impressed by her learned arguments or not, he devoted a great deal of space to them when he came to write his *Historia Calamitatum*. That she failed to move him is certain. And when she realized she had failed to win him to her point of view by intellectual reasoning, she turned away from her role of Hypatia to the humbler and more moving role of a mistress who fears for her lover's safety and her own.

Weeping now, she said that it would be highly dangerous for Abelard to take her back to Paris with him. She would be much safer in Brittany with his family. Why did she need to be called his wife, she demanded, when she found it sweet enough to be called his mistress? In one case, love alone would hold them together, in the other, only a chain.

"Even if we should be parted from time to time," she argued, "the joy of our meetings would be all the sweeter by reason of its rarity."

But no woman's arguments ever stopped a man from doing what he considered the right thing to do for her, once he had made up his mind. Abelard was as firm in his decision when she finished her pleading as he had been before she began. He was determined to make Heloise his wife whether she wanted to be or not. Perhaps—who knows—he was all the more determined because she did not want to be.

And at last, Heloise, realizing she could not move him, and unable to bear the thought that she might offend him, ended her protest, and with tears in her eyes, said, "Then there is no more left but this—that in our doom the sorrow yet to come shall be no less than the love we two have already known."

"Nor in this speech," Abelard wrote, "as the whole world came to know, was the spirit of prophecy lacking."

Because we have only Abelard's brief statement, in the story of his calamities—"And so, commending our infant son to my sister, we returned secretly to Paris"—one can only imagine the anguish it caused Heloise to part with her child. Although Abelard may have assured her that as soon as the secret wedding was performed, and Fulbert satisfied, she could return for her son, Heloise had already expressed a premonition that things might not be as easily accomplished as he believed they would be.

And yet, whatever the pain at leaving her infant child, so great was her love for Abelard that she would have as obediently laid down her own life had he demanded it of her. To return to Paris, to face the uncle she had so grievously wounded, required a tremendous amount of stoicism, but to part with the little son, born of her love for Abelard, required much more. She went along with Abelard, but her heart was heavy with the premonition that only sorrow lay ahead for all of them.

The journey from Nantes to Paris, partly by boat, partly on horseback, took several days. When they arrived, as by agreement, Heloise went to her uncle's house in the Rue des Chantres, and Abelard to his lodgings in the Latin Quarter.

In order to prepare themselves for the holy sacrament of marriage, in accordance with the ritual of that time, they spent long hours of vigil and prayer in "a certain church," and at last, one morning at daybreak, while the rest of Paris was still asleep, Heloise and Abelard were married in the presence of Canon Fulbert and a few chosen friends who were sworn to secrecy.

Immediately after the ceremony, Heloise and Abelard were parted, he to return to his lodgings and to continue his teaching at the university, and Heloise to the house of her uncle, whom she distrusted and feared even more than before. And so once again she was virtually a prisoner in the narrow house on the Rue des Chantres. Only now, added to her longing for Abelard were her uneasiness over her child and the ignominy of her position, which necessitated living a lie for Abelard's sake.

With the practical good sense of the Frenchwoman—which Heloise was "down to the last millimetre of her shadow," as Henry Adams has said—she realized it would be impossible to keep any secret in the small world that was the Paris of her day. Everyone knew now that Heloise and Abelard had returned to the city, and was speculating about why they had done so. And even if Fulbert had any intention of keeping his word—which was doubtful—the temptation would be too great for him not to let slip a hint of the marriage to some of his colleagues—in order to save his own face as well as to protect his niece from further calumny. And who could prevent the servant in the house from gossiping, since no one had thought to swear him to secrecy too?

And so, of course, the news of the marriage leaked out, just as Heloise knew it would. When she discovered this, she turned on her uncle in a small fury and, accusing him of breaking a most sacred vow, told him that she would denounce the tale-bearers and swear up and down, by all that was most holy, that no such marriage had ever taken place.

Infuriated at what he considered the last straw, all the past grievances that Fulbert had endured came to the surface. He struck his niece repeatedly, and ordered her confined to her room until she should recover a sense of obligation to him and respect for his word. From then on his treatment of Heloise was harsh, and he heaped punishments upon her until life became unendurable for her in his house.

When news of this treatment reached the ears of Abelard, he managed to help Heloise escape one day when her uncle was absent. He took her first to his own lodgings, although he knew that it would be impossible for her to remain there without all Paris knowing of it, in which case there would be no use denying that they were wed.

One wonders why Heloise did not return to Brittany, where she would have been safe from her uncle and with her child. Instead, and for whatever their reasons, it was thought that the rumors could best be stopped by Heloise returning to the convent of Argenteuil.

Abelard's plan, conceived in desperation, was for Heloise to put on the garb of a nun, except for the veil. Thus everyone, including Fulbert, would be forced to believe that Heloise had entered the order, and that Abelard had rid himself of her with finality.

If Heloise protested against this fantastic plan, there is no record of it. She knew it was born of Abelard's desperation, and she would have done anything to put his mind at ease and to protect him.

The nuns at Argenteuil received their child with open arms. However they may have felt about the deception Heloise asked them to perpetrate for her sake, they agreed to it. They understood that she was in trouble and had come to them for help. They knew that she had reason to wish to leave the outside world for a while, and lovingly they received her in their midst again.

Often, when rumors had seeped through the walls of the convent like poisonous vapors, the nuns had prayed for Heloise, that she might be restored to virtue in the eyes of God and the saints. And often they had mourned for their child who had met love so soon and so painfully. Therefore they rejoiced that she had come back to them of her own will, and they made a place for her that she might join her prayers with theirs.

And so, wearing the plain black gown of the order, with a white linen wimple covering her lustrous brown hair but no black veil over this, Heloise dwelt with the nuns, sharing their lives to a certain point, yet remaining apart from them by reason of the vows they had taken but she had not.

As she walked along the banks of the Seine where the river was gentlest, or among the fruit trees in the cloister gardens, while the sisters were busy at their duties or devotions, she was reminded of the child she had been, innocent and filled with wonder at the beauty of the world. And now she was a woman, filled only with grief at the separation from her husband and her son.

So short a time had there been between the child and the

woman, how could there have been so great a change? What more could the future bring? She dared not think.

But her mind could not help dwelling on the future and its possibilities, as she walked by the river, or tended a rose bush, or when she knelt with the nuns in prayer, bowing her head and asking God to keep Abelard from harm when the nuns believed she was praying to be forgiven for her sins.

The longing for Abelard was like a fire inside of her, a hunger that had no appeasement, a desire so poignant and so consuming that it kept her from sleep at night, and, almost, during the day, from breathing.

And then, as we know from his mention of it in one of his letters, Abelard came one day to see her. With what joy she greeted him, and with what tact and kindness the sisters left them alone for a brief while.

What happened then, when after the longing for each other and anxiety they were at last reunited, must seem to even the most indulgent a sacrilege. Abelard, unable to control his desire, and Heloise, not even then able to refuse him, or wanting to, they made of the cold stone floor of the nuns' dining hall a marriage bed.

Abelard, writing of this episode years later, has this to say: "Thou knowest how, after our marriage, when thou wert living in the cloister with the nuns of Argenteuil, I came one day to visit thee secretly, and what my ungovernable lust did with thee there, even in a certain corner of the refectory itself, since we had no other place to which we could withdraw; thou knowest, I say, how shamelessly we behaved in a place so holy, and consecrated to the Heavenly Virgin."

For this shocking deed they each had a lifetime of penance in which to atone. But we may believe that whatever Heloise and Abelard did in those troubled days was done not in the spirit of blasphemy, but because of their need to cling to each other. God had united them in marriage, and He was soon to part them forever. It was for God to judge them if, in the few precious moments they had left, they drew as close as possible to each other, in the only place available to them.

In the years to come, however much Abelard repented and beat his breast in shame over this act of lust, as he called it, Heloise was not ashamed of it. Their act had been one of love. God was love—and love made all things pure.

7

When Fulbert learned that Heloise was at Argenteuil, wearing the habit of the Benedictine order, he at once jumped to the conclusion that Abelard had tricked him. He quite overlooked the fact that, by failing to keep the marriage a secret as he had promised, he was in some way responsible for the miscarriage of all their plans. He was convinced that Abelard, regretting the loss of his career in the church, by marriage, had decided to rid himself of his wife by forcing her to become a nun, in which case their marriage was automatically dissolved.

Paris at that time was the seat of many rivalries and intramural feuds, and one can be sure that in university circles there were many who were jealous of Abelard and helped to fan the fury of anyone wishing to destroy him. With their encouragement, Fulbert swore he would be avenged for all that he had endured from Abelard, and particularly for what he claimed to be this final act of treachery.

It is highly probable that the original shock Fulbert suffered, when he first made the discovery that his niece had been seduced by the man he had so much admired and trusted, drove him to the brink of insanity. If so, this final act which he attributed to Abelard—the dissolving of a marriage that was to restore the pride of Fulbert's house—supplied the final pressure that sent him over the edge. Nothing now remained in that clouded mind except the will to destroy the man who had wronged him.

It is difficult to believe that the horrible means he took to achieve his revenge could have occurred to a mind that was not unbalanced. For the plan he conceived would destroy the marriage of Heloise more effectively than any supposed intention of Abelard. But Fulbert was beyond reasoning. All that he cared about now was to make Abelard suffer, to wound his pride as Fulbert's pride had been wounded—in a way that would prolong his suffering, a way that he diabolically decided would be more cruel than murder.

Fulbert laid his plans carefully. He chose a night when Abelard, after a particularly fatiguing day, had gone to bed exhausted. The servant who looked after Abelard had already been bribed to open the door and absent himself. Then Fulbert, some of his kinsmen, and a Spanish doctor entered Abelard's room, overpowered him as he half awoke from his deep sleep, and castrated him.

In the *Historia Calamitatum* Abelard described that night of horror: "The uncle and his kinsmen and associates, of the opinion that I had played a trick on them, and had taken an easy way to rid myself of Heloise by forcing her to become a nun . . . whereat vehemently indignant and conspiring together against me, on a certain night while I slept in an inner room of my lodgings, having corrupted a servant of mine with money, they punished me with a most cruel and shameful vengeance— to wit, amputating those parts of my body wherewith I had committed that of which they complained."

The morning after this outrage, the whole city of Paris gathered before Abelard's lodgings, shocked by the word, which had spread rapidly, of Fulbert's revenge. An account of this was given in a letter written by Foulque, the prior of Deuil: "The bishop and all the noblest canons of Notre Dame were shocked for Abelard and bewailed his fate. The women, whose idol he had been, wept for him as for a husband or lover killed in battle . . . and all the citizens of Paris mourned for the disgrace . . . which this had brought upon their city."

Of the crowds of sympathizers who swarmed the street before his door to commiserate with him, Abelard wrote: "It is difficult, nay impossible, to describe the amazement which transfixed them, the lamentations they uttered, the uproar with which they harassed me, of the grief with which they increased my own suffering. Chiefly the clerics and, above all, my scholars tortured me with their intolerable lamentations and outcries, so that I suffered more intensely from their compassion than from the pain of my wound.

"In truth, I felt the disgrace more than the hurt to my body, and was more afflicted with shame than with pain. My incessant thought was of the renown in which I had so delighted, now brought low, nay utterly blotted out, so swiftly, by an evil chance."

And yet, with all his misery, with all his anxiety for the loss of his glorious prestige, Abelard could write, although at a later date: "By how just a judgment of God was I stricken in that portion of my body wherein I had sinned!"

What consumed him, and ate into his soul, was the manner in which he believed the tale of his castration would be received by the world. With what joy his rivals would accept his disgrace! And what perpetual grief this stroke of fate would bring to his family and friends! But, oddly enough, of what it would do to Heloise he does not seem, at this point, to have given much thought.

What way would lie open to him now? he asked himself, as he writhed with shame. With what face would he appear in public, to be pointed out by every finger, gossiped about by every loose tongue, doomed to be a monstrous spectacle to all?

"Nor did it less confound me," he wrote, "that, according to the letter of the Law, that killeth, there is so great an abomination of eunuchs before God that men who have been made eunuchs by the amputation or bruising of their stones, are forbidden to enter the Church, as though they were unclean, and that in the sacrifice at the altar, even animals of that sort are rejected."

He then cited Leviticus, the twenty-second chapter and twenty-fourth verse, in which it is written: "Ye shall not offer unto the Lord that which is crushed or bruised or broken, or cut." And from the twenty-third chapter of Deuteronomy, he quotes: "He that is wounded in the stones, or hath his privy member cut off, shall not enter into the congregation of the Lord."

Concerning this reference to the Deuteronomic law barring certain unfortunates from the priesthood, some commentaries say that Fulbert, being aware of it, had perpetrated his deed in order to make sure that Abelard would never afterward be able to hold a high office in the church. However, these inferences are refuted by the fact that Abelard did later hold such a position, and, as abbot of St. Gildas, he even celebrated mass. In the necrology of Argenteuil, where the death of Abelard is recorded, he was described as a monk and priest of St. Denis.

It is believed that Fulbert lived for many years after the castration of Abelard, but that he was deprived of his property by the bishop and canons of Notre Dame. His accomplices and the faithless servant who helped perpetrate the deed were not only made to suffer the same mutilation they had inflicted, but had their eyes put out as well.

What happened to Fulbert after he was stripped of his house on the Rue des Chantres, of his precious library and his position at Notre Dame, is not known. Perhaps he became completely insane and was kept in a dungeon reserved for such unfortunates. Perhaps he died of old age and the bitterness of his memories, in the home of one of his unnamed, but frequently mentioned, kinsfolk. Or it may be that God, in His mercy, made Fulbert mad to an extent where all that remained in his memory was the face and form and voice of the gentle young girl who was entrusted to him, and who shared his love for Greek poetry.

There is no question but that the castration changed the course of Abelard's life, and no less so, that of Heloise. In the confusion of his shame, as he admitted later, rather than by devotion to the church, he was led to think of the retirement and seclusion of a monastic cloister. It was while he was contemplating such a step and before it was actually accomplished, that he thought of Heloise and what was to become of her. In his agony of mind at this time, there seemed only one course possible for her, as well as for him. He sent her a message that she was to take the veil at once, and join the convent of Argenteuil as a nun.

It is not known when or how Heloise had received the terrible news of her uncle's attack on Abelard. Unquestionably her first thought was to speed to her husband's side and to comfort him. Instead she was sent this peremptory message that made her natural wish impossible to fulfill.

All that she was able to do to prove her love was to follow Abelard's urgent command that she take the veil. And this, without question or without protest, she proceeded to do—as she would have gone to the scaffold for Abelard's sake, had he demanded it of her.

Some writers have accused Aberlard of ordering Heloise to become a nun before he had become a monk, because he was jealous lest some other man succeed him, since he was no longer capable of being her husband in the physical sense. But from all that is known of Abelard's character, that is improbable. It is more in keeping that he urged her to take this irretrievable step because he feared for her safety in case the wrath of her uncle should descend upon her too. As a nun in the convent of Argenteuil, safe in the arms of the church, she would be beyond Fulbert's reach.

There may have been other considerations too. Believing in this, his darkest moment, that he would no longer be able to look after Heloise if he were deprived of his remunerative classes, Abelard realized that as a nun her material as well as her spiritual needs would be met for the rest of her life.

There is little of this in the *Historia Calamitatum*. In fact, so concerned was Abelard with the account of his own miseries that he tells us nothing of the agony which the knowledge of his shame caused Heloise. Neither does he mention any meeting they had. It is left for us to imagine her distress, first at the mutilation of the body of her lover, and then at his determination to become a monk, a move which would deprive her of him forever.

More to her, though, than the loss of her beloved's presence was the manner in which the loss occurred. Knowing Abelard as she did, she understood the crushing blow to his pride and the agony of thwarted ambition that was his. And only she, in all of Paris, could understand that the mental torture was greater for Abelard than the physical, and why so much anguish could erase even the thought of her from his mind.

It is much harder for us to understand why, when he listed the causes of his grief, he never once mentioned the obvious result of his castration—that his relations with Heloise, his beloved and his wife, had come to an abrupt end. Nor did he mention any regret that, in becoming a monk, he would lose her forever. It is possible, of course, that the memory of their passionate love was bitter as gall to him. For had it not been the cause for that one quick deed which destroyed the whole carefully planned structure of his life?

And it may be that, losing no time in obeying Abelard's command that she become a nun—"*sans foi, sans amour, et sans espoir*"—and feeling herself to blame for his misfortune, Heloise wished to make a sacrifice in order to take upon herself some measure of punishment, that he might not bear it all alone.

When Heloise made it clear that she was renouncing the world for Aberlard's sake, and not for God's, some compassionate friends pleaded with her not to take so drastic a step—but in vain. How much easier it would have been for her if it had been for the sake of God, and to please Him, that she became a nun!

There is a story that, before taking the veil, Heloise broke down and recited these lines from Lucan's *Pharsalia*.

> Great husband, undeserving of my bed!
> What right had I to bow so lofty a head?
> Why, impious female, did I marry thee,
> To cause thy hurt? Accept the penalty
> That of my own free will I'll undergo . . .

The story is probably apocryphal, added by some chronicler who desired to give merely another example of Heloise's scholarship. It is easier to believe that her emotions were too deep for anything but silence at so solemn and irrevocable a moment.

In that moment, Heloise stepped to the altar, lifted from it the veil, and, before the bishop and the sisters of Argenteuil, publicly bound herself forever to the religious life.

A few weeks later, when he had recovered from his wound, Aberlard became a monk at St. Denis. With this step, he renounced the world, its glory, its pleasures, its fame, and its wealth.

With little appetite or fervor for Christian solitude, at first Abelard's mind was filled with inner torment and a desire for revenge. He blamed the weakness of Fulbert that permitted the old man to be influenced by Abelard's enemies. He accused these enemies for their complicity in the crime, rather than Fulbert. And he had an impulse to go to Rome to denounce them, and to ask for justice.

His friends succeeded in dissuading him, among them Foulque, that same prior of Deuil whose letter has been quoted. Such a voyage, Foulque said, would be folly. Abelard was now too poor for the costs of Roman justice and Roman cupidity. Also, he advised, it would be most unwise to alienate forever the head clergy of Paris.

And then, with the final thrust of truth, Foulque said, "Besides, my friend, you are no longer a private individual, you are a monk."

Not long after this, Abelard wrote: "The clergy, pouring in upon me, began to make incessant demands both of our abbot and of myself, that what I hitherto had done from desire for wealth or praise, I should now do for the love of God, considering that the talent which had been entrusted to me by God would be demanded of me by Him with usury, and that I who had aimed principally at the rich should henceforth devote myself to the education of the poor.

"And to this end chiefly, I should know that the hand of God had touched me, namely that being at last set free from carnal snares and withdrawn from the turmoil of secular life, I might devote myself to the study of letters. Nor should I become a philosopher of the world so much as of God."

This was good counsel, and well-meant. And yet—for Abelard who had been so proud and so free; for Abelard who had been so handsome and strong, quick-witted, impatient of fools and bores, possessed of a natural grace of manner that could charm every man and woman he met; for Abelard the maker of verses, the singer of songs, the lover of life and of beauty—it was the counsel of pity. And it tasted of wormwood—as he bowed his head in acceptance.

8

It was as we have seen, not unusual in the Middle Ages for married couples to separate and enter a monastery and a convent in order to seek individual salvation, or for any number of other reasons. It was a deeply religious age and an emotional one.

Had not Abelard's own parents done this very thing? Although still loving each other, from all accounts, each sought a way to serve God better by renouncing the worldly life. In their case, it was Berenger who first became a monk, and Lucie who followed his example. She was middle-aged by then, if not older. She had lived a very full life, bearing children and seeing them on their way; her cup was filled.

Besides, Berenger had always been devoutly religious, and so had his wife, Lucie. When they sought the cloistered life it was through conviction, and not from necessity; from the desire of their hearts, and not *faut de mieux* or because no other way lay open to them.

Heloise, on the other hand, was still very young when she became a nun at Argenteuil. She was still at the threshold of life and the world. What was more, she had never shown any real religious vocation, either as a brilliant little girl at the convent school or later.

And yet Abelard had imposed this sentence upon her: that she shut the door on the world forever and devote herself to prayer and contemplation for the rest of her days.

Young and passionate as Heloise was at this time, the step

she was to take for Abelard's sake was a cruelly difficult one. We know this from the letters she wrote to him much later. But her inner struggles with her conscience and her true desire were not so much caused by rebellion against Abelard's decision, but by rebellion against God for taking this drastic way of leading them to the religious life.

The one person who could have consoled her at this point, who could have given her the moral help she desperately needed, was Abelard. And yet there is evidence that he, who had once overwhelmed her with love letters and poems and songs of praise, now did nothing to help or encourage her, either, as she wrote, "by talk . . . or by letter." Abelard was too lost in his own misery.

In spite of this, Heloise was able to walk to the altar and place the veil upon her head. And no one saw her weep or heard her complain. "Her soul was Roman and her heart was a heart of fire," someone has said. And another writer, Enid McLeod, calls it "a Roman valor of soul, a kind of antique sternness against which nothing could prevail."

Heloise was nineteen when she became a nun. She had been out in the world barely two years before she met Abelard, and all that had happened from the time that she met him took only eighteen months. For this one brief interlude Heloise had lived as other women, and then the world was snatched away from her again. And once more her life became measured by the bells for prayers and the duties she was called upon to perform. But where formerly there had been the hope of escape into a more normal life, now there was no such hope: no escape at all for the rebellious heart, except the ultimate ones of resignation—or death.

It is a well known fact that for an intellectual female, the convent offered the very best opportunity to continue her studies. But Heloise was a woman in love with a man, and no course of study seemed to her a compensation for the loss of her lover. What joy could she have in the thought of perusing the convent's treasury of books—while her mind was still filled with the sound of that one beautiful voice?

Heloise conducted herself in such a way that she won the respect and affection of all who were near her. She spent many hours alone in her cell, meditating—asking God to give her the strength to keep her vows; repeating that most poignant of prayers: "God, I believe. Help Thou my unbelief!"

If she were also penitent, asking to be forgiven her sins, it would have been easier for Heloise. Those hours spent in solitary contemplation would have had a pattern, the pattern of all sinners seeking redemption: *Mea culpa, mea culpa, mea maxima culpa*.

But it is not on record that Heloise believed that loving Abelard, with all her heart and soul and body, had been a sin in the sight of God. He, who was aware of her innermost thought, would know that all she had done had been done through love. There could be no evil, no sin in love.

And so, believing this, how could she pray for forgiveness? Instead, her prayers were to be granted a better understanding of why she and Abelard had been punished. Why, she asked, if other men and women were permitted to live together in health and happiness, must she and her lover be condemned to live apart for the rest of their natural lives?

"Teach me, help me to understand! Show me how to live with my sorrow, and how to fulfill Thy purpose. Strengthen Thou my weak knees, that I may not sink under the weight of my grief and that of my beloved's. Teach me how to live without him—and how to accept Thy will with grace." Thus Heloise prayed.

We know that she was granted the strength and the grace. In the ten years that she remained at Argenteuil, before she went on to found a new convent, her behavior was exemplary and earned her the highest praise from those who were closest to her. But of the struggle within, of the dark moments she faced alone in her cell, of the temptation to cry aloud and rebel against her fate, no one at that time had a word to say. Silently Heloise performed her duties, graciously she bowed her head and prayed with the other nuns. The sisters of Argenteuil had reason again to be proud of the lamb that had been returned to their fold.

The basic rule of the Benedictine order was employed by all the monasteries and convents of the twelfth century, although there were several outgrowths of the Order.

In his prologue to the rule, St. Benedict wrote: "Hearken, my son, to the precept of the master and incline the ear of thy heart; freely accept and faithfully fulfill the instructions of a loving father, that by the labor of obedience thou mayest return to him from whom thou hast strayed by the sloth of disobedience. To thee are my words now addressed, whosoever thou mayest be that renouncing thine own will to fight for the true King, Christ, dost take up the strong and glorious weapons of obedience. . . .

"Let us, therefore, gird our loins with faith and the performance of good works, and following the guidance of the Gospel walk in his paths, so that we may merit to see him who has called us into his kingdom. . . .

"Therefore must we establish a school of the Lord's service, in founding which we hope to ordain nothing that is harsh or burdensome. But if, for good reason, for the amendment of evil habit or the preservation of charity, there be some strictness of discipline, do not be dismayed and run away from the way of salvation, of which the entrance must needs be narrow. But as we progress in our monastic life and in faith, our hearts shall be enlarged, and we shall run with unspeakable sweetness of love, in the way of God's commandments; so that, never abandoning his rule but persevering in his teaching in the monastery until death, we shall share by patience in the sufferings of Christ, that we may deserve to be partakers of his kingdom."

". . . ut ab ipsius numquam magistero discedentes, in ejus doctrina usque ad morte, in monasterio perseverantes passionibus Christi per patientiam participemur, ut et regni ejus mereamur esse consortes. Amen.

The *Regla* of St. Benedict gave the most detailed commands for the monks' conduct and occupation for each hour of the day and night. (These same rules applied to nuns as well, although St. Benedict used the word monk exclusively.) According to the rule, there was to be no time left unguarded, but the monk was to be kept so busy with righteous acts and thoughts that there would be no leisure for sin. The commands of what not to do are comparatively unemphasized. The monk is guided along the right paths rather than forbidden to stray.

In the fourth chapter of the rule for monks, St. Benedict lists "the tools of good works" (*quae sunt instrumenta bonorum operum*). First come the Ten Commandments, and then appear the following rules:

> To deny oneself, in order to follow Christ.
> To chastise the body.
> To relieve the poor.
> To clothe the naked.
> To visit the sick.
> To bury the dead.
> To help the afflicted.
> To console the sorrowing.
> To avoid worldly conduct.
> To prefer nothing to the love of Christ.
> Not to yield to anger.
> Not to nurse a grudge.
> Not to hold guile in one's heart.
> Not to make a feigned peace.
> Not to forsake charity.
> Not to swear, lest perchance one forswear oneself.
> To utter truths from heart and mouth.
> Not to render evil for evil.
> To do no wrong to anyone, and to bear patiently wrongs done to oneself.
> To love ones' enemies.

This is only a partial list of the rules that both Heloise and Abelard followed. Perhaps, in their grief, they found it good to have a light to lead them out of the darkness. But for Heloise, there was always one "tool of good works" that she had difficulty in applying: "To prefer nothing to the love of Christ." Only in this did she make a feigned peace.

9

In spite of the rules of St. Benedict, there were, in the Middle Ages, some badly run monasteries, just as there were bad monks and nuns—human nature being what it is.

Abelard had chosen the abbey of St. Denis because it was the most important in the kingdom. And he was received there with enthusiasm, not only for his family name, but because his prestige as a scholar would bring glory to the community of monks.

Crippled as he was by the unspeakable thing that had happened to him, Abelard was seeking only silence and forgetfulness. He was quite prepared to renounce the world forever, and to follow the rule of St. Benedict to the letter, as well as in spirit. He was, in fact, almost eager to fulfill the duties that the abbots had indicated, and to occupy himself with the poor who came to St. Denis for instruction.

But this rich monastery in which Abelard found himself was, as St. Bernard once said, "more devoted to Caesar than to God." It was worldly, and was joined to heaven by the merest thread. Irritable as well as saddened by his misfortunes, Abelard could find there little of the peace he was seeking.

"Now this abbey of ours," he wrote, "to which I had repaired, was entirely abandoned to the secular life, and that of the lewdest. Whereof the abbot himself exceeded the rest of us no more in rank than in the dissoluteness and notorious infamy of his life. Their intolerable filthiness I frequently and vehemently attacked, sometimes in private, sometimes publicly, thereby making myself burdensome and odious beyond measure to them all."

The standards set by St. Benedict were high, and it is not to be wondered that some monks, even an abbot, fell short of them. Not only St. Denis, but other monasteries of the day were accused of shortcomings. To name a few of them: frivolity instead of earnestness; gluttony instead of fasting; avarice instead of charity and almsgiving; lustfulness instead of chastity; pride and vainglory instead of meekness.

One of the critics, although he appeared on the scene a little later, in the thirteenth century, was Eude Rigaud, archbishop of Rouen. He visited some monasteries and convents where he found nothing to reform, but he recorded "abominable conditions" in others. One entry of his reads as follows.

"*Calends of October, 1248.* We are again at Ouville. We found that the prior wanders about when he ought to stay in the cloister; he is not in the cloister one day in five. *Item,* he is a drunkard, and of such vile drunkenness that he sometimes lies out in the fields because of it. *Item,* he is incontinent, and is accused in respect to a certain woman of Grainville, and also with the wife of Robertot, and also a woman of Rouen named Agnes. *Item,* brother Geoffrey was publicly accused with respect to the wife of Walter of Esquaquelon who recently had a child with him. *Item,* they do not keep proper accounts of their revenues. *We ordered that they should keep better accounts.*"

Abelard made no specific accusations against the monks of St. Denis, but merely mentioned conditions of filth and lewdness. There is no doubt, however, that he could make himself very unpopular when he chose, and that far from continuing as an object of pity, he lost little time making new enemies.

However disgusted he was, however uncomfortable he made those around him, and no matter how they retaliated in kind, what concerned Abelard most was the effect these conditions had upon his teaching. He finally persuaded the abbot to allow him to draw apart from the brethren, to a certain cell, in order to conduct his school in the manner in which he had formerly conducted it.

When the students of France heard that Abelard was teaching again, they came to him for instruction in such numbers that the space allotted to him was not large enough to contain them all. Whether he continued to teach the poor, as had been his new intention, we do not find mention. But we do know that he was supposed to confine his instruction to the Holy Scriptures, and that Abelard, no matter how honest his intentions, was unable to lay aside entirely the secular subjects in which he was more fully versed, and which the students demanded of him. (In combining both secular and religious teaching he was following in the footsteps of Origen, one of the Greek fathers of the church, who had written many works on the Old Testament, and who used, so he claimed, instruction in secular philosophy as a bait to draw students to the study of church history.)

At any rate, what followed was the same thing that had happened before. Abelard succeeded in drawing pupils away from other classes to his own, thereby arousing the jealousy of the other masters. Two of these, Alberic and Lotulph, who had already displayed their animosity toward Abelard, were the first to be aroused. They were ambitious to take the places of the defunct masters, William and Anselm, and they now feared that Abelard would spoil their chances.

This was exactly the sort of opposition that had always acted as a spur to Abelard, and he soon revealed that whatever changes had occurred in him physically, he had not changed intellectually.

According to some authorities, Abelard now left St. Denis, and entered the priory of Maisoncelle, situated on the estate of the count of Champagne. Here he established a school to take care of the thousands of students who came clamoring to him for instruction. He taught theology, but also philosophy, in accordance with Origen. This return to the teaching of philosophy was the weapon which his enemies, led by Alberic and Lotulph, now used. They attacked his methods and also questioned his right to return to secular teaching, now that he was a monk.

Abelard, overjoyed to find that he had lost none of his ability to captivate an audience, attempted to ignore his critics. For a brief time he even deluded himself that he would be able to continue his glorious career. The respect and encouragement of his students helped him to believe this, and to ignore the unhappy fact that "a strength once interrupted does not ever again find itself as strong," as an admirer of his ruefully observed. It also helped to hide from him the funereal shadow that had fallen across his future.

Pressed by his students, Abelard soon reduced the number of his lectures on theology, forgetting that he had sworn to instruct only in the philosophy of religion. He even wrote a treatise for his students on the nature of God, that is to say, on Unity and the Divine Trinity. He called it *Introduction to Theology*. It endeavored to demonstrate faith by reason—for those students of his who were "demanding rather what could be understood than what could be stated, saying indeed that the utterance of words was superfluous unless first it had been understood, otherwise it would be 'the blind leading the blind.'"

Basically, Abelard's most important message was that Christianity may be combined with human reason. He had no desire to do more than give to man the right to love God in his own soul. However, the Holy Ghost, at that time, was a most sensitive subject with the church and its dignitaries. And Abelard could not refrain from dwelling on it to some extent. It was enough, apparently, for any point to be tender in order that Abelard should wish to attack it!

He intended to say nothing heretical, nothing that was not already implied in the church's teachings, although what he said was said brilliantly. In fact, he treated the subject with almost exaggerated respect, but he would not let it alone!

As long as Abelard merely lectured, he was not stopped. But when he began to write treatises such as the *Introduction to Theology*, his enemies immediately seized upon them to denounce Abelard to the higher authorities, and he was summoned to appear before a council to be held at Soissons. He was ordered to bring his tract with him.

The charges that his enemies (Roscelin, Alberic, Lotulph, and other former champions of William of Champeaux and

Anselm) brought against Abelard were that he had preached
and written that there were three Gods!

So successful had Alberic and Lotulph been in spreading lies
about Abelard among the clergy and the people, that when he
arrived at Soissons with a few of his pupils, he was actually
stoned by some of the populace. Seeking out the papal repre-
sentative, Abelard handed over his tract for the legate to read,
declaring that if anything be found in it that dissented from the
Catholic faith he would readily correct it or give satisfaction.

He was instructed to take the book to the archbishop and to
his two rivals, that they who were his accusers might judge him,
that it might be fulfilled: "even our enemies themselves being
judges." However, when he presented the book to Alberic,
Lotulph, and the archbishop, they, unable to find anything in it
that they dared present at the hearing, moved that the reading
be postponed to the end of the hearing.

The council continued for several days, on each of which
Abelard publicly expounded the Catholic faith just as he had
written it in his tract, winning the admiration of his audience
by his use of words and the sense he expressed. Abelard had
lost none of his eloquence or his appeal, apparently, and soon
the tide of opinion swayed toward him. The people began to
ask, "Of what does he stand accused?"

His rivals, quick to notice the climate of public opinion going
in Abelard's favor, became more and more enraged. And one
day Alberic approached Abelard, with evil intent but a bland
manner, saying that there was one thing he marveled at in the
book, namely that, "whereas God begat God, and there was but
one God, Abelard had denied that God had begotten himself."

To which obscurity, Abelard replied, "On this point, if you
wish, I will reason."

"We pay no heed," Alberic said pompously, "to human reason, nor to our own sense in such matters, but only to the words
of authority."

"Very well then," said Abelard, quickly, "turn to the page in
the book where I have given the authority." And there being a

copy at hand, Abelard found the place, which Alberic had chosen to ignore, and there was a sentence which went:

"*Augustine On the Trinity*, Book I, Chapter 1. 'Whoso supposes God to be so powerful as Himself to have begotten Himself, errs the more greatly in that not only God is not so, but no creature, either spiritual or corporeal. For there is nothing whatsoever that may beget itself.'"

While others who heard this had the grace to blush, Alberic, recovering himself, murmured, "It is well that it should be understood." But still angry, he resorted to open threats, assuring Abelard that neither his reasons nor his authorities would help him at this trial.

When the last day of the council arrived, the legate and the archbishop, before they even took their seats, began to discuss with others what should be decided about Abelard and his book, this being the reason they had been called together. They all seemed undecided, because so far they had found nothing in what Abelard had said to make him seem guilty of heresy.

Geoffrey, the bishop of Chartres, addressed the others, saying: "All of you who are present here know that this man we are asked to judge has, by his teachings and his intellect, many supporters. His fame has spread over the world, from sea to sea. If you condemn him because, whatever the reason, you have been prejudiced against him, you will offend many people. He will not be wanting in defenders, and you must take care lest you confer more fame upon him by any violent action on our part, especially if the charge is false.

"If, however, you are disposed to act in accordance with canonical law, let his dogma and his writing be brought before us, and let him be questioned and allowed to answer freely, that he may convict himself, or, confessing his error, be forever after silent."

But Alberic and Lotulph cried out that no one could withstand the rhetoric of Abelard if he were allowed to speak for himself, forgetting, as Abelard brought out later, that it was more persuasive to hear Jesus Himself when He was living, and yet Nicodemus had insisted that He be heard according to law.

When the bishop found that he could not induce Abelard's rivals to consent to his proposal, he tried by another suggestion to curb their vindictive desire that Abelard be punished for heresy. He proposed that the present council was too few in number to judge so weighty a matter, and that Abelard should be heard at St. Denis, his own monastery, before the abbot and a larger number of learned persons. There it should be decided what was to be done in the matter.

To Abelard's rivals such a decision would mean that they had achieved nothing. If the matter were carried out of their diocese, they would not be allowed to sit in judgment. So they hastened to the archbishop and persuaded him that it would be a reflection on his own powers if the case were to be transferred, and that it would be most dangerous to all if Abelard were to escape punishment.

They then persuaded the legate, in spite of his reluctance, that he should condemn the book without any inquiry, have it burned in public, and to have Abelard confined to perpetual retreat in some obscure monastery. The arguments they put forward were that Abelard had ventured to read his tract publicly without being authorized by the Roman pontiff or by the church, and that he had given it to be copied by many scholars. It would be of great benefit to Christianity, they argued, if a similar act of presumption were prevented by making an example of this one.

The bishop of Chartres, who was friendly to Abelard, and who foresaw that the legate and the archbishop would be convinced by these arguments, advised Abelard to accept the sentence quietly, since there was no doubt that the cruel and unfair decision would only reflect against his enemies and win him more friends in the long run. Furthermore, he was not to worry about confinement in a strange monastery, since the legate, who was being compelled to act by his superiors, would eventually set him at liberty, as soon as the smoke had cleared away.

"And so he gave me what comfort he could," Abelard wrote, "and to himself also, both of us in tears."

Abelard was called before the council on this last day at Soissons and, without any further pretence of a trial, was ordered to cast his book in the fire that had been built for the purpose. "And thus it was burned," Abelard wrote, "when, in the silence that fell on all the onlookers, one of my adversaries was heard to murmur that he understood the book to say that God the Father alone was Almighty."

And the legate said he marveled that any little child should make such an error, when the Common Faith held that there are three Almighties.

Then Terric, a schoolmaster, quoted from the creed of Athanasius: "Yet there are not three Almighties but One." And when the bishop took him to task, he recited the words of Daniel: "Thus ye foolish children of Israel, neither judging nor knowing the truth, ye have condemned the daughter of Israel. . . . Return to judgment, and judge the judge himself."

Then Terric went on: "This day, by divine mercy, deliver him who is plainly innocent, like Susanna, from his false accusers."

But the archbishop rose, confirming the legate's sentence, saying, "The Father is Almighty, the Son is Almighty and the Holy Ghost is Almighty, and whoever dissents from this is in error." He then suggested that Abelard be asked to expound his own faith before all, that he be either approved or corrected, as was fitting.

When Abelard rose quickly to profess his own faith, his enemies prepared a new indignity for him. They declared that it would be sufficient if he recited the Athanasian Creed—which any schoolboy of the day could have done. And to make the humiliation ever greater, they placed the written words before Abelard, as if he did not know them.

With bowed head, Abelard read as instructed, following which he was publicly handed over to the abbot of St. Médard, and committed to his cloister, as though to prison. After which the council was dissolved.

The monks and the abbot of St. Médard were delighted to have so eminent a scholar in their midst. They felt that he would attract followers, as he always did, and thereby bring many benefits upon their humble monastery. They tried to console him for his recent disgrace, and meant, no doubt, to be helpful and kind. But Abelard was not to be comforted.

He kept to himself, remaining most of the time in his narrow cell, reflecting on his wrongs and the injustices that had been heaped upon him. With great bitterness he repeated the cry of St. Anthony: "Good Jesus, where wert Thou?"

Compared to the way Abelard was now suffering, the injuries that had been inflicted upon his body were as nothing. Those he admitted he was able to endure because he had deserved them. He had committed a grave sin with his mortal body, and he had been punished, as was fitting.

But this injury to his pride went far deeper than the wound to his flesh. It hurt the more because he felt it was undeserved, and because it attacked the very foundations of his faith. No further proof than this is needed to reveal that Abelard's pride in himself was an intellectual pride only. Nothing, before or after the bestial attack on his manhood, counted as much to him as the humiliation he had just been made to endure before an assemblage of his so-called peers.

Although it was little comfort to him now, what the bishop of Chartres had predicted came true. Public opinion turned against those who had acted so unfairly and cruelly at Soissons. Those who had acted against Abelard through spite and jealousy now repudiated their responsibility and accused each other. Even the legate, in an effort to exonerate himself, publicly deplored "the jealousy of the French."

One result, however, of the legate's regret for the part he had played in the trial was that he arranged for Abelard to be moved from the abbey of St. Médard and allowed to return to St. Denis. This was, as it turned out, a dubious blessing.

At St. Denis there were no open arms waiting to receive Abelard. Instead, he was met with coolness and hostility. He had so constantly reproached the monks of St. Denis for what he called the vileness of their lives and the shamelessness of their conversations that they were hardly overjoyed at his return to their midst. They used every possible means to make him un-comfortable, and even, he insisted in the *Historia Calamitatum*, went so far as to mutter threats against his life.

It is possible that Abelard's misfortunes had affected his sanity, and that he was suffering from delusions of persecution. He makes frequent reference to his fear of attacks on his person, and seems to have seen enemies lurking in every shadow in the cloisters. But then it is wholly possible that the enemies were real, since Abelard, in spite of his cowl and his fall from emi-nence, was still determined to express his disapproval when it pleased him to do so, and being intolerant, still made enemies easily.

At last the trouble at St. Denis came to a head. One day, as he was lecturing to his students, he happened to refer to a pas-sage in Bede's commentaries on the Bible, which declared that Denis the Areopagite was bishop of Corinth and not of Athens. Now Denis was the patron saint not only of all the Gauls but of the monastery in which Abelard was staying. And since he was called the Areopagite from the famous tribunal in Athens, the brethren to whom Abelard half-jestingly cited this contrary opinion of the Venerable Bede, were highly indignant.

They declared Bede to be a mendacious writer, and offered instead the testimony of their own abbot, Hilduin, who had traveled in Greece and had in his opinion, established the fact that St. Denis had been bishop of Athens. They challenged Abelard to decide between Bede and Hilduin. Abelard replied that the authority of Bede, whose writings the entire body of the Latin churches consulted, seemed to him the more ac-ceptable.

Whereupon the brethren, violently incensed, cried out that now Abelard had shown that he had always been an enemy of their monastery and, not only that, had attempted to detract from the honor of the whole realm by denying that their patron saint had been the Areopagite.

Abelard replied calmly that he had not denied it, nor was it of any great importance whether Denis had come from Athens or elsewhere, since he had won so bright a crown before God.

But the monks hastened to their abbot and told him what Abelard had said. And the abbot, who had been severely criticized by Abelard and who feared him because his own conscience was troubled, was delighted to find an occasion whereby he could make trouble for this annoying monk. He called the entire chapter and all the brethren together, and threatened Abelard openly, announcing that he would send him immediately before the king of France to answer for this insult to their patron saint.

At first Abelard offered himself to the discipline of the monastery, if he had in any way offended, but this was refused him. But one night, certain that the whole world was conspiring against him and horrified at the villainy of those among whom he was living, Abelard managed to escape, with the help of a few monks who took pity on him.

He made his way to the neighboring lands of Theobald, Count of Champagne, who had shown himself a friend on other occasions and now offered Abelard sanctuary in the town of Provins with some monks of Troyes. The prior had once been a bosom friend of Abelard's, and still loved him dearly. He made Abelard welcome and tenderly cared for him.

Now it happened that the abbot of St. Denis came to the town of Provins to transact some business with Count Theobald. Abelard, hearing of this, went to the count and asked him to intercede with the abbot and request that Abelard be given permission to live in whatever monastery he chose. This the count did, but the abbot of St. Denis, fearing that it might reflect on his own monastery if Abelard chose to live elsewhere, refused the count's request. He added that if Abelard did not return to St. Denis, he would be excommunicated, as would the friendly prior if he continued to shelter him.

This was disturbing news, and things might have gone badly for both Abelard and the prior had not the abbot been suddenly stricken, a few days after his departure, with an illness from which he died en route to Paris.

The person to succeed him as abbot of St. Denis was no other than Suger, adviser and favorite of Louis VI. Abelard lost no time in applying to him for permission to teach without being connected with a monastery. Now both Suger and Louis, occupied as they were with political matters, were only too glad to rid themselves, as they thought, of the troublesome Abelard. In their opinion, the less regular an abbey was, the more profitable it would be to the king in temporal wealth. But, lest St. Denis should lose prestige if Abelard's scholarship and fame should benefit another abbey, they agreed to permit Abelard to move to whatever wilderness he chose—provided he placed himself under the protection of no other monastery. This was agreed upon in the presence of the king and his council.

And so Abelard, a monk, and poor, but on his own now, retired to Troyes on the banks of the Arduson River, a deserted place which he knew and where he had once gone to read and to enjoy solitude. It was in the parish of Quincey, near Nogent. Here, on land given him by a friendly baron, with the permission of Atton, bishop of Troyes, Abelard built for himself an oratory of reeds and thatch. He named it "The Paraclete," the Comforter—in honor of the Holy Ghost.

Here, hidden from the world with one of his disciples, he wrote that he could truly say, with the Lord, "Lo then did I wander far off and remain in the wilderness."

10

During those years which Abelard described in the *Historia Calamitatum*, from the time he became a monk of St. Denis to the time he established his lonely oratory in about 1128, there is no mention of Heloise.

What happened to her during those ten or more long years can only be determined from the records of the convent of Argenteuil, of which none remain except an obituary roll believed to have been written by the hand of Heloise. Not only did this roll follow the traditional formula, but it contained an elegy in Latin which, it is said, no one at Argenteuil at that time would have had the erudition to compose save Heloise. It was written with a feeling for and an understanding of the rhythm and grace of Latin verse and with a distinction that causes scholars to believe it hers. And, since it was not the custom to give so important a task to an ordinary nun, this is one of the proofs offered to establish the fact that Heloise was abbess of Argenteuil by the year 1129 at the latest, and probably a number of years before that.

This was a great responsibility for such young shoulders. Not only was she the head of one of the most important convents in all France, with the complicated business which that involved, but she was also the moral and spiritual leader of women older than herself.

According to the rule of St. Benedict, the abbess was to be an example to the other nuns, "displaying goodness and holiness by deeds and by words." She was to be kind as well as stern, not closing her eyes to faults, but seeking to help her sisters rather than to rule them. Her role was to be that of mother, rather than superior officer. She was expected to be a leader, one who would bear responsibility, and set the spiritual climate of her convent.

Although, in a way, the abbess was a sovereign, when any important business was transacted she was required to convoke the whole community of nuns and ask each, from the oldest to the youngest, to express an opinion. After the matter had been fully discussed, however, the abbess had to make the final decision alone.

Having to make final decisions and bearing so much responsibility at so early an age resulted unquestionably in the strengthening of Heloise's character. The passionate, impressionable young girl that she had been became a more reserved, thoughtful, and serious woman, who used her authority with justice and wisdom.

To act as an example to the other nuns meant that she could show not one vestige of the anguish that was tearing at her heart. To show her grief would have been a sin.

But it was a sin even to feel such grief. She was to acknowledge no other love but that for God and His Son. The apostle John had said: "God is Love; and he that dwelleth in love dwelleth in God, and God in him." John had not meant, and Heloise knew it, love such as she still bore for Abelard. That love had been conceived in passion and expressed in the passion of a healthy woman for a man she adored.

But no amount of prayer or mortification of the flesh could assuage her mortal hunger for the presence of her beloved husband, for the touch of his hand, the pressure of his lips, or for the ultimate gratification of a desire that was still a smoldering fire waiting to burst again into flame.

There was the example ever before her of the founder of her order, Benedict of Nursia. While he was still young and living in the desert, he was beset with frightful temptations. The world he had so recently left still dwelt with him in his mind, and he was haunted by the image of a woman he had once seen. The more his imagination dwelt on this image, the stronger grew his desire, and he had almost reached the point of leaving the desert and returning to the life he had abandoned when he noticed a clump of thorns beside him. Taking off his clothes, he flung himself amid the thorns and wallowed in them until his flesh was torn to ribbons. And thus by the wounds of his body he was cured of the wounds to his soul. Only by using this cruel method was he able to conquer carnal desire.

There were no thorn bushes in the carefully tended gardens of the convent cloister. If there were, it would not have been becoming for the Abbess of Argenteuil to fling herself among them. Heloise had to bear her torment in silence and with fortitude, knowing it to be a punishment which she had to accept, without any redeeming sublimation.

"There is no fear in love, but perfect love casteth out fear: because fear hath torment. He that feareth is not made perfect in love." —And there was not a moment of her long day but Heloise feared for the safety of Abelard. She was without any reassuring news, only such fragments as were carried to the convent by others—and these only fed her misgivings and her genuine concern.

Not only was it difficult to bear this lack of direct news of Abelard, but, during the hours when she observed silence in her cell and gave herself over to meditation, she was forced to accept that most humiliating of all conclusions—that Abelard's love for her had been merely lust; that once desire had been killed in him by his emasculation, he no longer felt anything for her at all, not even ordinary kindness.

If it had been anything but lust, she asked herself, would he not have concerned himself more deeply for her welfare all these years, than only to have arranged for her to be confined in a nunnery for the rest of her life? Had he not cut himself off from all communication with her, as if he feared to be contaminated by the least thought of her who had, unwittingly, brought about his ruin?

These were bitter thoughts to live with, yet Heloise lived with them in silence and became all the stronger for them. St. Benedict had once said to a monk who suffered a mishap: "Work on and be sad no more."

So Heloise worked very hard and strove by her industry and her example to make the convent of Argenteuil grow, not only in wealth and prestige but in piety and good deeds. This was not easy—even for one who had adopted the holy way of life through conviction rather than circumstance.

There were many rules set down by Benedict which were difficult enough for the monks he had in mind when he wrote them. They were even more difficult for women who entered the order. The rule of chastity may have been easier for the sisters to obey than for the brothers, but the rule of total renunciation of personal property was not. By personal property was meant not only valuable assets, such as lands and serfs and castles, but the merest trifle—a book or a tablet or a pen, even a pet such as a cat or a dog or a caged bird. For some reason, the nuns had a very hard time obeying the rule about pets!

In one of his complaints against a certain nunnery—not Argenteuil—Rigaud reported that on a visit of inspection it was found that "they kept little dogs, squirrels, and birds. We ordered that all such things be removed." These same nuns mentioned in Rigaud's record, were also reproved for having locked chests. Their abbess was instructed to inspect the chests often and "unexpectedly," or to take off the locks. She was ordered to take away the nuns' girdles that were decorated with embroidery, their fancy pouches, and the silk cushions on which they were working.

In cases of such infringements of the *Regla*, Heloise was less strict than she might have been. If she was, as Henry Adams claimed, *tout-ce qu'il y a de Francaise*, that is to say, "a French-woman to her fingertips," then she was a woman with fine common sense, as well as a warm understanding for the little foibles of the human race, especially those of her own sex. She was the last to deny her nuns the comfort of befriending and owning some small animal, both for the animal's sake and for the nuns'. She knew too well the ache of emptiness, the need to be loved and to love that could not always be met by prayer and fasting.

Carrying a sense of guilt herself for not being able to live up fully to the rules of St. Benedict, it is unlikely that Heloise was overly strict with the guilt of others. In a meaner nature, the reverse might have been the case—for some of us it is almost impossible to forgive that sin in others which we are struggling, in vain, to conquer in ourselves. But there was no meanness in Heloise. If she was strict with her nuns, it was where strictness would help to run her convent more efficiently; that the nuns might perform fruitful work and be better equipped to help the needy, who often demanded food and clothing and prayers for their souls.

Under Heloise, the convent of Argenteuil, which had always been one of the richest in Europe, prospered and brought increased revenue to the church. The land was fully cultivated and produced not only sustenance for the convent but vegetables and fruit to be sold at a profit. The barnyards supplied fat calves and pigs, for meat, and the dairies supplied milk, cream, and butter. The nuns, obedient to the dietary rules of their founder, ate sparingly, and mostly of fish which were drawn from the Seine. Surplus food which was not sold was given away to the needy.

There were also vast tracts of woodland belonging to the convent, far beyond the needs of the nuns for winter warmth or the construction of outbuildings. These woodlands, or forests, brought in a not inconsiderable amount of wealth to the order.

Heloise, young as she was in years, and brief as had been her experience in the outside world—which could have included no commerce whatsoever, and very little exchange of money—managed to handle the affairs of the convent like an astute businesswoman. This earned for her the respect and approval of those who were interested in the prosperity of the church property for its own sake. Alas, it also attracted interest for other reasons.

Heloise was, for all her outstanding independence of mind, a product of her own age, even though she now belongs to all the ages. In the twelfth century, and even earlier, women played an astonishingly prominent role in the affairs of their day. We tend to remember, when we consider the role of women in the Middle Ages, such things as the chastity belt, one of which is still a popular exhibit at the Cluny Museum in Paris. These were locked on their wives by suspicious husbands before they went off to fight in the Crusades, to hunt, or to explore new horizons. But we are apt to overlook the fact that while their husbands were away, these same wives had to rule their sometimes vast households, or conduct the family business, whatever it happened to be.

Both physically and mentally, the women of the twelfth century were as robust as the men. They even dressed more or less alike. Men parted their hair carefully from the crown to each side of the forehead, and sometimes their locks grew as long as a woman's. Their slippers had pointed toes that turned up at the tip, and their robes swept the floor, often in trains. They wore gloves and adopted a number of other fashions that would seem to us the prerogative of the feminine sex. These fashions in dressing, and in behaving, however, did nothing to detract from their ability to fight fiercely or to make love to their wives, or their mistresses, with enthusiasm. But they did demonstrate an equality between the sexes that extended in a number of directions.

For one thing, the ascendancy of women was even more pronounced by their close attachment to the all-powerful church. With husbands and fathers away so often and for such long periods of time, it fell upon wives and mothers to instruct the young sons in religious matters, and to keep up the family's religious obligations.

It was in the twelfth century, moreover, that the cult of the Virgin began to reach its greatest and fullest expression. As Henry Adams has pointed out, men flung themselves at the feet of woman (the Virgin) rather than man (Jesus). It was she who represented their hope for the future. She alone represented the kind of love they could understand. The Trinity could, by its nature, administer justice. But Mary gave them hope. She was human, like themselves, someone who could understand their language and accept their excuses. The literature of the time is filled with stories demonstrating the compassion of the Virgin toward poor, miserable sinners.

There is the familiar tale of the nun, for example, who left her convent for a night and returned in the morning, ready to accept her punishment—only to find that no one knew of her absence because the Virgin had descended from her niche and had carried on the duties of the nun until her return.

In a collection of medieval mystery plays, called *Les Miracles de Nostre Dame*, there is the story of the pious woman and her knightly husband who, from devotion to the Virgin, took a vow of continence. One night the husband, incited by the devil, persuaded his lady to forget her vows. When she discovered, subsequently, that she was to bear a child, the wife was so chagrined at her broken vow that she offered the infant to the devil. When, after its birth, the devil arrived to claim his own, the whole machinery of the church was set in motion. The case was eventually brought before God, where the devil pleaded on one side and *Nostre Dame* pleaded on the other. Our Lady won, on the strictly practical grounds that a mother could not give her offspring to the devil without the father's consent, which in this case had not been given.

To his contention that women were the equal of men in the Middle Ages, Henry Adams added the observation that it was always the woman who seemed to keep her head, even in affairs of the heart. The man was always getting himself into trouble, into crusades or feuds, or debt, and depending on some woman to get him out of the mess.

Heloise, fortunately for her, belonged to that century in which women, through the Virgin, played so prominent a role. In a darker age, or a more puritanical one, she might have been lost among sinners, the brightness of her mind ignored, the selflessness of her love discounted. Instead, she lived in a time that built such wonders as the cathedral of Chartres as a tribute to a woman, a sign of worship that elevated the whole sex. Unfortunate though she was in so much else, she was fortunate at least in this.

11

At first, after he had found a hiding place in the wilderness near Troyes, Abelard lived alone with one of his clerks who had insisted on remaining with him. They had built their oratory with their own hands, and they lived on what they could find to eat in the woods or in the stream.

Abelard does not say whether, in this interlude, he found the peace of mind he was seeking. But, surely, after being harassed on all sides by real and possibly imagined dangers, he was glad to live apart from other men, if only to clear his own mind.

And yet he found it necessary to defend his withdrawal from the world: Had not the Pythagoreans chosen to dwell in the wilderness and the solitary places? he asked. Had not Plato, a rich man by all accounts, preferred a villa far from the city, in a spot not only remote but unhealthy, in order that he might find no delight but in study? Had not, in fact, St. Benedict and other saints chosen a desert wilderness, the better to pursue God?

But whatever reasons Abelard gave for choosing so isolated a spot in order to be alone, the world soon sought him out. When news of his retreat reached the scholars, they began coming to him from all parts of Europe, to live near him in the wilderness, and to beg him to conduct a school again.

At first Abelard refused them and remained aloof. But still they came, leaving the cities; willing, even eager, to live in little reed huts they constructed themselves; eating herbs and roots and wild berries, and sleeping on straw—ready to endure any kind of hardship in order to be near the master.

For a man whose pride had been so broken, this tribute was inordinately comforting. For a man who was born to teach and to whom silence was death, it was surely a cup of water offered in Christ's name. Humbly he accepted the cup, and began to teach again.

However, by his own admission, it was not entirely the importunities of the scholars that drove Abelard to conduct his classes at this time. Unaccustomed as he was to hard, manual labor, he couldn't dig in the fields as many a hardier monk could do. Nor could he, without embarrassment, set out with a bowl or an extended palm and beg for alms as others before and after him could do. In order to supply his daily wants, he was forced to use the means that were his—the clear mind, the gift of oratory, and that most rewarding of talents, the ability to teach others.

Abelard's students paid him in various ways. They tilled the fields so that there was food for him and for them. They also enlarged the oratory, building with stone and with timber, so that it grew from an unsightly temporary shelter into an actual monastery, still crude but at least bearing a resemblance to other abbeys.

When Abelard first established his little chapel in the wilderness, he was a fugitive and in despair. In gratitude for the grace of divine comfort that had been granted him here, he decided to name the place after the Divine Comforter, and so he had called it the Paraclete. (The word itself is Greek, meaning an advocate, one called to aid or support, hence a consoler, comforter, or intercessor. But the term, in the twelfth century, had also come to mean, when capitalized, the Holy Ghost.)

Thus Abelard, although perhaps unwittingly this time, once again laid himself open to attack by his enemies. They claimed to be shocked that he had dedicated his oratory to the Holy Ghost, since it was customary to name churches and monasteries after a saint or the Trinity, or to dedicate them to the Son or even the Father—but never to the Holy Ghost alone!

Abelard answered his critics by saying that he had called his oratory after the Comforter, and he quoted the Apostle, who said: "Blessed be God, even the Father of our Lord, Jesus Christ, the Father of mercies and the God of all comfort; who comforteth us in all our tribulation." And he also reminded them of the promise: "And He shall give you another Comforter."

But there are people who always seem to embrace the unpopular side of arguments, and this was so of Abelard throughout his entire career. It was true that he had named his sanctuary after the Comforter, who had delivered him when he was cast out by his enemies. The gesture was one of pure gratitude, a genuine outpouring of love for the Spirit that had given him this place where he might pray in peace and work for the glory of God. However, in the twelfth century, among many sensitive points of doctrine, this one of the Holy Ghost was one of the most tender, the sorest. It seems unfortunate that, just when Abelard needed friends and supporters more than ever, he should have pressed against this sore spot and aroused the interest and attention of those powerful ones of whom, for his own safety, it had been wiser to remain out of sight and mind.

More than once in his stormy career, Abelard had stirred up trouble for the sake of argument, which he enjoyed. This had certainly been true of the young Abelard, fearless and bold. Now, trouble had not blunted the keenness of his mind, but one would think it might have made him more careful in wielding its blade.

However, instead of letting the matter fade away, as it might have done, Abelard insisted on continuing to defend his choice of a name for his small abbey. Day after day, instead of lecturing on the place of logic in philosophy, or on any other of his usual subjects, Abelard lectured his students on why it was fitting to ascribe a temple or altar to the Holy Ghost.

And with every protest, the length and depth of the enmity he incurred within the church was increased. And these enemies were not all to be despised, nor were they to be easily appeased by Abelard's brilliant arguments. Some of his enemies were very powerful, and some were extremely popular. The strongest and the most popular was Bernard, the abbot of Clairvaux—he who was in time to be called St. Bernard.

Bernard was born at the end of the eleventh century, of a noble Burgundian family, just as Abelard was born of a noble family of Brittany. There were other similarities. Like Abelard, Bernard was handsome, gracious of manner, and persuasive of tongue. Both received the best education available in that day and age. But here the similarities ceased.

Abelard's approach to Christianity was intellectual, Bernard's emotional. Where Abelard was satisfied to let others think and believe as they saw fit, as long as they used their brains, Bernard was anxious to persuade others to think as he did, and capable of going to extreme, even cruel lengths to carry out the task of converting them.

Abelard's contribution to the world has been summed up by a French scholar, Mme. Guizot, in her *Essai sur la vie et les ecrits d'Abelard et de Heloise,* as follows: "What Abelard taught that was most novel for his age was liberty, the right to consult reason and to listen to it alone. An almost involuntary innovator, he had methods that were even bolder than his doctrines, and principles whose range far outran the consequences at which he himself arrived. Hence his influence is not to be sought in the verities he established, but in the impulse which he gave.

"He attached his name to none of those powerful ideas which act throughout the centuries, but he imparted to minds that impetus which perpetuates itself from generation to generation."

Of what use, Bernard asked, was philosophy to him? His teachers were the apostles. They had taught him not "the art of using the syllogisms of Aristotle." "What Peter and Paul taught," Bernard said, "was how we ought to live." An intellectual himself, as a matter of fact, it pleased Bernard and suited his purpose to belittle the tendency to "be always learning and never arriving at a knowledge of the truth."

Bernard, unlike Abelard, was a natural ascetic. In his youth he was subjected to the usual temptations of the flesh, but he made the decision early that his life must be one of absolute continence. It is said of him that one night a harlot came to his bed and lay down beside him, but that Bernard's only reaction was to move over and make room for her, and then to turn on his side and continue his peaceful sleep. It is small wonder if he found it impossible to understand, much less condone, the passion of Abelard for Heloise.

When Bernard made the decision to enter a monastery, he might have applied at the monastery of Cluny, which was even then rich and important, and was far more lenient than some others. It was to Cluny that most noblemen and their sons came when they chose to adopt the monastic life. Instead, Bernard chose the more austere Cistercian order, which consisted, mainly, in a personal reliving of the Gospels.

One day in the year 1112 Bernard and thirty companions, some of whom were his own brothers, applied for admission at the little monastery of Citeaux. Here the rules of St. Benedict were rigidly enforced, and here Bernard remained for three years until he was ordered to start his own chapter house on the property of the count of Troyes.

He chose a tract of land known as "the valley of absinthe," and changed the name to Clairvaux, "valley of light." The monastery he erected on this site became popular under his rule, and the very austerity Bernard enforced seemed to attract rather than discourage new members. All of his monks suffered extremes of cold and hunger. They made soup of green leaves, and often had only acorns to eat, but they had the inspiration of Bernard, who taught them by his own example.

It is said that Bernard fasted so much he ruined his health, subduing his body without mercy. He slept in a wretched cubicle in which he couldn't stand up without hitting his head against the beams of the ceiling, and, for a pillow on which to rest his head at night, he used a straw-covered block of wood.

Most of the young men who flocked to Bernard came from the noblest families of France. When parents became afraid of his influence, and shrank from his approach, Bernard said to them, "Do not shed tears for your son, he is going from sorrow to joy. I will be father, mother, brother and sister to him!"

Eventually Bernard's impulse to direct the lives of others led him into politics, so that he made his influence felt not only in monastic affairs but in affairs of state. As early as 1124, when Honorius II became Pope, Bernard was invited to share in ecclesiastical councils. At the synod of Troyes, to which he had been invited, Bernard obtained recognition for a new order called Knights Templar, which he helped organize in France, and whose purpose, briefly put, was to protect the Crusaders on their way to and from the holy land.

After the death of Honorius II, Bernard succeeded in getting Innocent II elected pope. From that time on, Bernard was accompanied on many of his travels by Pope Innocent, who also spent much time at Clairvaux. It is also said of Bernard that he had great influence with King Louis. It is true that he did have enough weight with the king to persuade him to undertake the Second Crusade, and, when this crusade ended in disaster, far from being crushed by the outcome, Bernard began urging a third crusade to retrieve the losses. He even offered to lead this one himself, but the Cistercian abbots refused to allow such a sacrifice.

Bernard had many admirers in his day and afterward, though he was also severely criticized by some of his contemporaries. And even some of his admirers were forced to admit that the manner in which he hounded Abelard was a far cry from the saintliness for which he was known.

It is easy enough to understand why Bernard feared and hated Abelard, but it is unforgiveable that he should have implied conclusions which Abelard had never drawn, or that, not satisfied with disputing the ideas of his opponent, he sought to attack him personally.

For example, in a letter to Pope Innocent II, Bernard wrote: "Peter Abelard is trying to discredit the Christian faith when he deems himself able by human reason to understand God. He ascends to heaven and even descends to the abyss. Nothing may hide from him in the depths of hell or in the heights above! The man is great only in his own eyes—this scrutinizer of Majesties and fabricator of heresies!"

Bernard, who sought to reach God through ecstasy and love,

could not be expected to approve of the methods used by Abelard, much less Abelard's conviction that doubt was a necessary stage through which men had to pass before they discovered God. "Who can endure this cold?" Bernard demanded.

But was this a reason to accuse Abelard of "speaking iniquity openly?" or of "corrupting the integrity of the faith and the chastity of the church?"

Yet Bernard goes on to say of Abelard: "He oversteps the landmarks placed by our fathers in discussing and writing about faith, the sacraments, and the Holy Trinity. He changes each thing according to his pleasure, adding to it or taking away from it as he sees fit. He is a man who does not know his own limitations, making void the virtue of the cross by the cleverness of his words. Nothing in heaven or on earth is hidden from him —except himself."

Perhaps Bernard really believed these accusations to be true. But it is easy to understand why Abelard should have been a thorn in the flesh to Bernard from the very beginning. Certainly, he disapproved of Abelard's treatment of William of Champeaux. And he was most certainly scandalized at the seduction of Fulbert's niece, and horrified by the manner of Fulbert's revenge. All of this was quite enough to turn Bernard against Abelard.

But now, as if matters were not bad enough, there was the actual presence of Abelard, teaching his "heresies" in a spot that was only fifty or sixty miles from Clairvaux, where Bernard was exemplifying and teaching an entirely opposite spirit of religion. In fact, the Paraclete was on a direct line between Clairvaux and its father house, the abbey of Citeaux, near Dijon. If Abelard had deliberately set out to find a spot as close as possible to the heart of church activity—even though to all appearances it was still a wilderness when he chose it—he could not have hit upon a more central location.

There is little reason to doubt that Bernard was one of those "former rivals," of whom Abelard speaks in his *Historia Calamitatum,* who went about the world preaching and slandering him in whatever way they could, charging monstrous things not only against his faith, but against his manner of life. They succeeded in detaching from Abelard some of his principal supporters, and even some of those friends who preserved their affection for Abelard were afraid to show it.

"God is my witness," Abelard wrote of this period of his life, "that I never heard of the summoning of an ecclesiastical assembly without feeling sure that its object was to condemn me."

In this Abelard was not far from the truth. But, however deeply the Cistercians disliked Abelard and feared him, it is to Bernard's credit that no violence was committed against him. A much subtler method was devised to get him out of the way. They enlisted the patronage of the church and, through the church, the state to insure his silence.

One of the most powerful figures in France at this time was Abbot Suger, who was adviser to both Louis VI and his son, Louis VII. Officially, he was head of the important abbey of St. Denis, and as such, Bernard was quite proper in consulting him about the best plan to get the annoying Abelard out of the way.

Suger came up with a brilliant idea. An abbey in Brittany, St. Gildas, had just lost its abbot. And at a hint from Suger, the monks of St. Gildas requested that Abelard be selected to take his place. Since Abelard had been a monk of St. Denis, this seemed to be perfectly in order.

Suger, furthermore, being a politician, offered the post to Abelard as a signal honor, emphasizing the point that as abbot of his own established monastery, he would be equal in rank with Bernard and with Suger himself.

Abelard was well aware of the reasons for his removal from the Paraclete. He was tempted to refuse the honor that they wished to confer upon him, but Suger intimated that he would do well to accept, because there was no alternative.

"Thus," Abelard wrote, "the jealousy of the French drove me to the west as that of the Romans drove Jerome to the east. For God knows I would never have acquiesced in this except that I might escape oppression. . . . So, like a man who, terrified by a sword that is hanging over him, dashes towards the precipice, and by avoiding one death incurs another, so I from one danger bore myself . . . often in my prayers repeating the words, 'From the end of the earth will I cry unto Thee, when my heart is overwhelmed.'"

There is no doubt that this "honor" which the church, by way of Suger, offered to Abelard was equivalent to banishment or worse. St. Gildas was situated on the wildest part of the coast of Brittany, although it was only seventy miles, more or less, from Abelard's birthplace. The country was barren and savage, and the people spoke in a strange tongue. The abbey was built on a cliff that made it seem to Abelard like a prison, with the ocean around it cutting off escape. The winters were bitterly cold, and the fierce winds that swept over the place were a constant reminder of the coldness and cruelty of those who sought to restrain not only his body but his mind.

Even more than the starkness of his surroundings, what was hard for Abelard to endure was the depravity of the monks whom he was supposed to instruct and control. The depths to which they had sunk caused him anguish, lacerating his soul by day and by night. He was convinced that if he tried to correct them or compel them to lead the ascetic life they professed, it would cost him his life, and that if he didn't attempt to reform them to the extent of his power, it would cost him his soul.

St. Gildas was in the domain of a certain Duke Conan who ground down the monks with heavier extortions than if they had been vassals. Some of the monks had private means which, instead of turning over to the monastery, they kept for themselves. Others committed a little extortion of their own among the neighboring peasantry. With these private funds they bought wine enough to get drunk on, and supported concubines and their offspring.

As their abbot, Abelard was now responsible for feeding the monks. There was little food to be found in that savage countryside, and even if the ground had been more fertile, none of the monks would till the soil. Every day, however, they came to Abelard demanding to be better fed, although they knew how short were the supplies. Not only that, but they often stole what little there was in the larder. There was no one outside the monastery walls to whom Abelard could appeal, since the duke was as depraved as the monks within, and was too busy plundering his neighbors to be approached.

Abelard's account of the miseries he endured at St. Gildas sounds at times like the figment of a mind suffering from a form of paranoia. And yet it is possible he was giving a true description of the perils he underwent. He firmly believed that the monks over whom he was supposed to preside were attempting to poison him. But even the founder of his order, St. Benedict himself, had made similar charges against certain monks of his day.

It has been said of Abelard that a greater career in the church was opened for him when he became abbot of St. Gildas, and that if he did not die an archbishop it was not entirely the fault of the church. He was already a prelate equal in rank to Suger of St. Denis, Peter the Venerable, of Cluny, and Bernard of Clairvaux. It may be true that if he had been a politician, as were those others, he might have gone far and become wealthy and powerful. But Abelard was no politician.

There is no suggestion of any such eminence in Abelard's story of his calamities. There is, rather, a strong note of self-pity, and of almost cringing humility which contrasted sharply with the character of a younger Abelard. The proud stallion was now, indeed, a gelding. He loathed the place in which he found himself master against his will. He felt he had been cruelly used and that the whole world was in a conspiracy against him. But worst of all was the degree with which his conscience tortured him because he had abandoned the Paraclete and those of his followers who had trusted him and depended on him for their instruction and salvation.

He wrote: "I considered, weeping, how useless and miserable a life I was leading, and how fruitless to myself and to others. I thought how I had formerly profited my clerks, whereas now that I had deserted them for the monks, neither in them nor in the monks was I bearing any fruit, and how impotent I had proved in all my undertakings and endeavors, that now it might be most properly said of me by all men: 'Abelard began to build and was not able to finish.'"

12

One of the deepest causes for regret that plagued Abelard now was the knowledge that the Paraclete had been abandoned by him, and that the offertory stood neglected. This problem was soon to be solved, but in a way that made it seem, at first, another calamity rather than the blessing it proved to be.

Into that cold northern country where Abelard sought to bring order and reason, although his soul was sick with discouragement, came the bitter news from Paris that the nuns of Argenteuil, over whom his own Heloise presided, were about to be evicted from their convent and sent out into the streets to beg for their food and lodging.

For all his preoccupation with himself and his troubles, Abelard had never actually been indifferent to his wife's welfare. If he kept himself away from her, was that not the proper conduct under the circumstances? One of the causes of his despondency, even if a minor one, was that there was nothing more he could do for his wife. Was it not best for her to forget him—if she could? He had not written to her. What could he write about except those things which would cause her more pain? It was more merciful to keep silent.

Despite the lack of personal communication, Abelard was informed of the way things were going with Heloise. The fact that this news was brought to him before the expulsion took place is proof of it. Therefore, had there been a breath of scandal, Abelard would surely have heard. Instead, the reports that reached him were full of praise for the good works performed by the abbess of Argenteuil, under whose administration the convent had become richer and more influential for good than almost any convent in France.

Heloise herself had grown in wisdom as well as virtue, paying heed to the exhortations of Paul, who warned his disciples to abstain from all appearance of evil, as well as from evil itself.

In the prologue to his *Regla*, St. Benedict had written: "First of all, whatever good work thou undertakest, ask Him with most instant prayer to perfect it, so that He who has deigned to count us among His sons and daughters, may never be provoked by our evil conduct. For we must also so serve Him with the gifts which He has given us, that He may never as an angry father disinherit His children, nor yet as a dread lord be driven by our sins to cast into everlasting punishment the wicked servants who would not follow him to glory."

No matter what the reason that had led Heloise to take the veil, during these ten long years she had given ample proof of her obedience to God, as well as to St. Benedict. She had known the warfare with oneself that is called grand. Her own conduct was above suspicion, nor did she permit the conduct of her nuns to be otherwise.

There were, nevertheless, forces at work beyond her convent's walls over which Heloise had no control. One of these forces was jealousy; the other was greed.

The Abbot Suger was an ambitious man. But, as adviser to Louis VI and his son after him, he was ambitious for them, for the crown of France, rather than for himself. One reason that the king was willing to trust the royal business to Suger was just this—that he had no private interests.

Suger was of lowly birth and undistinguished appearance. He was short of stature and prematurely bald. But he was extremely shrewd. Having had a hand in removing the troublesome Abelard from the Paraclete to the equivalent of Outer Mongolia, this new step he was to take represented a further intention to persecute the recently appointed abbot of St. Gildas. It is much more probable, however, that he was motivated by strictly mercenary and materialistic designs.

Desirous of increasing the temporal wealth of his own abbey, St. Denis, and thereby the wealth of the king, Suger cast an envious eye upon the prosperous convent of St. Marie at Argenteuil, just around the bend in the river. How convenient— if somewhat surprising after so much time—it was for him to remember that Argenteuil, or rather its convent, had once belonged to the abbey of St. Denis. And thus, having established the fact that the nuns were "trespassing," it was but a short step to ask for their expulsion that they might be replaced by monks.

Without too much difficulty, Suger produced a document to support his claim. He professed to have discovered a charter of the founding of the convent, in which it was said that from the time of King Pepin it had belonged to the abbey of St. Denis. He did not mention, although he must have known of them, other documents which showed that the convent at Argenteuil had been founded a hundred years earlier than Pepin, in the reign of Clothair.

There was no one strong enough or influential enough to step forward with proof that Suger had doctored, if not conjured up, his evidence. And yet, Suger must have been aware of the insubstantiality of his claim. Not only that, he knew that public opinion would be critical of him if he used so obscure a claim to turn over to his monks a place that had been for so long a religious retreat for women. He therefore looked around for other means to achieve his end without incurring adverse criticism.

There was one way this could be done, and Suger was not above stooping to use it. He proceeded to attack the morals of the nuns of Argenteuil in a manner so violent as to astonish everyone—including historians.

There is a document, drawn up in 1129 by the papal legate, Matthew, bishop of Albano, in which is recorded what happened at an assembly of ecclesiastics, including the archbishop of Rheims and the bishops of Paris, Chartres, and Soissons, in the presence of King Louis VI, Suger's friend and confederate. They had met ostensibly to consider the general reform of monasteries in France. This document describes the following scene which took place:

"Suddenly, there was an outcry, in the hearing of everyone, against the irregularity and evil repute of a certain monastery of nuns called Argenteuil, in which a few nuns living in manifold infamy, to the dishonor of their order, had by their impure and disgraceful ways for long defiled the whole neighborhood of that place."

The document goes on to suggest that at this assembly, on the mere claim set forth by Suger, plus the sudden outcry against the nuns' immorality, (an outcry which could very easily have been raised by a claque Suger had planted in the audience) it was decided that St. Denis should take over the convent at Argenteuil, and that arrangements should be made immediately for the dispersal of the nuns.

When Suger placed these same charges before the pope, along with the charter which he had so miraculously dug up, the convent and its adjuncts, he wrote, "were restored to St. Denis. As much because of the justice of our cause as because of the irregularity of the evil lives of the nuns there."

There is no indication that any attempt was made to inquire into the truth of these serious charges, or that any careful examination was ever made of the documents Suger put forth to press his claim to that rich plum which he coveted, not for himself, but for his king. Nowhere, either, is there to be found a suggestion that the nuns were given an opportunity to defend themselves against the vile accusations, or allowed to submit any document of their own to prove their right to possession. Surely, if such an opportunity had been given, Heloise would have been well qualified to come to her own defense and that of her nuns.

It is strange that neither in the *Historia Calamitatum* nor in the exchange of letters between Abelard and Heloise is there found any mention of the accusations. There is only the item of news conveyed to Abelard at St. Gildas to the effect that the nuns of Argenteuil were to be expelled from their convent. This could mean that Heloise and Abelard were kept in ignorance of the charges, or else that they considered them so absurd and unwarranted that neither thought them worthy of mention. Still, it is hard to believe either that they did not know of the causes of the expulsion or that those two, who were so outspoken concerning everything else in their lives, should have shown any reticence about this.

Whatever the cause of their silence, it is still impossible to believe that Suger's charges against Heloise and her convent were based on any truth. From every other source, including Peter the Venerable of Cluny, one finds nothing but the highest praise for the Abbess Heloise. The slander must have been fabricated by Suger merely to substantiate his false claim to the property which was to add to the revenues of his king. The reputation, happiness, or lives of a handful of nuns would have meant nothing to a politician like Suger.

There is, however, a very good reason why this seeming catastrophe brought forth no cry of indignation, no loud protest, even if such were possible, from the abbess of Argenteuil. Something of far greater importance to Heloise was about to take place. At last—at long last—she was to see her beloved Abelard again.

Had it been required of her that she walk through the flames of hell, she would have done so willingly, joyously even, that this result might be achieved—that she might see with her own eyes how Abelard, her husband, was looking, whether he had lost weight, or was too pale; that she might hear once again that beautiful voice speaking to her, even if the words that fell upon her ears were not those that had once brought her ecstasy, but quieter words with all passion gone from them.

All that she had prayed for in the loneliness of her cell, all that she had dared to hope for, was about to come to pass. She and Abelard were to be together again, if only for a few hours, a few days, a few weeks. The length of time could not be so important now, if only she could see him once again. That was enough. It was worth all that she had endured, all that Suger, the king, or the pope himself could do to her. Nothing in God's world or out of it could mean as much to Heloise as this.

Abelard, who had been "born again" by his suffering, both mental and physical, could never bring himself to admit openly that he was moved by the plight of Heloise and lost no time in coming to her assistance. What he did admit was the torment it had caused him, ever since he left the Paraclete, to think that he was unable to provide for the celebration of the divine office in the oratory he had built there—and how that problem was miraculously answered by the Comforter Himself.

"For it happened," he wrote, "that our abbot of St. Denis acquired by fair means or foul that abbey of Argenteuil wherein Heloise, my sister in Christ now rather than my wife, had taken the religious habit, as belonging by ancient right to his monastery, and forcibly expelled from it the convent of nuns over which my comrade held the priorship. When these were scattered in exile to divers places, I realized that an opportunity had been furnished me by the Lord whereby I might provide for our oratory.

"For returning thither, I invited her with certain others of the same congregation who had clung to her, to the aforesaid oratory. And they being conveyed thither, the oratory itself with all things pertaining thereto, I surrendered and gave to them, and that donation of mine, with the assent and by the intervention of the bishop of the place, Pope Innocent II corroborated to them and their successors by privilege in perpetuity."

In his life of Abelard, de Remusat somewhat puzzlingly suggests that Heloise and Abelard did not meet at this time: "*Peut-être même à son silence est-il permis de croire,*" he writes, "*que tous ces arrangements se conclurent sans que les deux epous fussent un moment reunis.*"

How could he have concluded that all arrangements were made without the lovers being reunited for a moment? Did not Abelard write that, returning to the Paraclete, he invited Heloise and certain others there, and that "they being conveyed thereto" he surrendered to them the oratory and the lands that surrounded it, as a gift?

By his very reticence in the matter, it is possible to assume how deeply moving to both Abelard and Heloise that first meeting in ten years must have been. In spite of the changes that had taken place in him, the hardships he had undergone, and the weight of the years that had been added, Abelard could not help but be stirred at the sight of Heloise. She was no longer the slim girl he had once known and passionately desired, but a beautiful and serious woman of twenty-nine, whose devotion to him had survived the lonely years and the heart-breaking silence he himself had imposed.

As for Heloise, how poignant it was to see again the one being whose welfare meant more to her than her own life, more than the whole world. And how anxiously she observed the changes in him.

The Abelard she saw now was not that handsome, arrogant, and fearless young man who had laid violent siege to her body and her mind; the ardent lover whose desire for her had swept them both beyond the threshold of sense and reason into a heaven they shared and then into separate hells. He was not even the protective yet stern husband who had ordered her, for her own safety, or so he thought, to take the veil. This Abelard whom she met again, at last, in the forsaken oratory by the banks of the river Arduson, in the wilderness near Troyes, was a man whose beauty of body had been broken on the rack of persecution and disgrace. This Abelard, whom she longed to enfold in her arms, or, better still, be held in his, that the terrible ache might at last be assuaged—this Abelard whom she saw was thin, weak, and emaciated by fasting and indifference to the needs of his body. This Abelard was a monk, an ascetic, in whose eyes she could read now only compassion for one who had shared his own calamities.

This is how it is recorded: "In the year 1129, the abbot of St. Gildas gave to Heloise, his sister in orders, his fellow worker in the Christian Church"—the only thing he had left of value to give, a little oratory of sticks and stones called the Comforter, a few acres of wilderness, and a place to lay her head.

It was a gift of love, no matter what reasons he chose to ascribe to the act. It was a proof of his concern for her welfare.

And as such, Heloise, no matter how great was her hunger for more, accepted the gift.

In her thoughts that day, never expressed in words, lay the promise that under her supervision the Paraclete would be forever after a haven, not only for her and her little band of nuns, but for Abelard—a place of refuge where he could be safe from the fears that she sensed haunted him now by day and by night.

The Paraclete, she promised in that silent vow, would be Abelard's as long as it was hers, and for this reason she would work to make it great.

13

In the *Historia Calamitatum*, Abelard writes that he was criticized because he gave less help and succor to the poor nuns of the Paraclete than he could and should have done. Therefore, he says, he began to visit them more often, in order to help them in whatever manner he could.

If this is true, it is difficult to understand why Heloise, in her letters later on should have reproached Abelard for failing to do this very thing; or why de Remusat should have said that they did not meet at this crucial period in their lives.

If we are to believe Abelard—and why should we not?—then for the aid and advice he gave Heloise and the little band of nuns, he must have received in return the balm of adulation and praise which was heart-warming to him, and the tender care for his physical needs that had been neglected for so long. Tormented as he had been these past years by the hatred and jealousy of his fellow men; afraid that whatever he ate or drank might be poisoned by the very monks whose souls he wished to save; misunderstood by his peers; hounded and calumniated on all sides, what a relief it would have been to find himself among those who loved him and from whom he had nothing to fear.

And yet those very voices that had been raised in criticism of him for neglecting the poor nuns now criticized him even more openly for helping them. Abelard wrote that now his detractors "with their accustomed depravity," accused him of using the welfare of the nuns as an excuse for rejoining his wife and, surprisingly enough, of having carnal relations with her.

A philosopher of Abelard's stature should have known that slander is usually stupid, and ignored it. Yet he gave an inordinate amount of attention to these rumors, and to proving them groundless. One explanation for his obsession with this foolish gossip may have been that he wished to protect Heloise, who had already suffered enough from the malicious calumnies of Suger.

Why, Abelard demanded, when divine mercy had set him free from suspicion of lewdness; when the means of perpetrating any such act had been taken from him, should he still be accused of visiting his wife in order to cohabit with her?

"For the state in which I am," he wrote, "so removed the suspicion of lewdness from all men's minds that those who seek to keep a stricter watch over their wives attach eunuchs to them." Elaborating on this, he gave several examples of eunuchs, including Origen, the great religious philosopher who, when he undertook the instruction of women in sacred matters, "laid violent hands upon himself."

Had not Pope Leo IX, replying to the Epistle of Parmenian, said that it was not lawful for bishop, priest, deacon, or subdeacon to cast away his wife from his care for the sake of religion, or not to bestow on her food and raiment, but only that he should not lie with her carnally? Was not Abelard trying to comply with this pronouncement?

Yet the criticism of him grew to such an extent that it could not be disregarded. His visits to the Paraclete grew less frequent, his manner to Heloise colder and more distant. And when this did not stop the slanderous tongues, Abelard's visits ceased altogether.

Did he tell Heloise his reasons for ending his visits? Or did he say *adieu* one evening and vanish down the road from the Paraclete, his form draped in the habit of his order, the cowl drawn over his head, his bare feet in sandals that scattered the dust, while Heloise watched him from the grille of the doorway?

During those visits, he had mentioned to her his fears for his life. And not all of those fears were the product of an imagination grown morbid through sorrow, since it has been recorded that an actual attempt to poison Abelard was made by the vindictive monks of St. Gildas. Heloise knew this. His withdrawal now was all the more cruel, since her worries for his safety were increased.

If there was such a thing as punishment for the sin which in her own heart she had never yet acknowledged a sin, then this was it—to long to help and comfort the man she loved, to offer him safety and peace, and to be denied the right to do so.

It was not easy for Heloise and her small band of devoted nuns to survive much less to build, in those early days at the Paraclete. And yet they did both. Their life at Argenteuil seemed pampered to them now as they applied themselves to unaccustomed labor in the fields and in the kitchen, with tools that belonged more properly in the hands of men or domestic servants.

Now it was not enough, as it had been, to fulfill the duties of devotion, to recite the prayers for the hours of lauds, prime, terce, sext, none, vespers, and compline; or, by rising at midnight, to perform the night office. What was needed here at the Paraclete was the pulling up of sleeves, the tying on of aprons, and the wearing out of knees in hard, earth-bound labor. There was need, also, for intelligence and courage. And Heloise had both of these.

At first they were left alone to struggle as best they could with the ordinary problems of survival. But before very long, those in the neighborhood who had feared scandal, having observed how serious were these nuns from Argenteuil, came to their assistance.

There was a certain lord of Nogent, Milo, who had given Abelard the original tract of land on which to build his oratory, and who, from his own personal resources, had added at least three fields already cultivated, the use of a forest to provide lumber for building and firewood, and also some marshland bordering the river. This same Milo now gave to the nuns, in addition to his original gifts, the sole right to fish in the stretch of the river between the towns of St. Aubin and Quincey.

Generous as those gifts were in the time of Abelard's residence at the Paraclete they had been barely sufficient to sustain a single monk. Now, even with the added fishing rights, they were inadequate for the needs of Heloise and her nuns. Suger, who had tacitly promised to look after and provide for those he had so ruthlessly expelled from Argenteuil, had not kept his promise. But there were others who took pity on these "poor handmaidens of Christ who, at the Paraclete, devoutly served God."

When the neighborhood learned how pious they actually were, not corrupt and abandoned to sin as was expected from the slanderous accusation by which Suger acquired their property in the north, gifts began to pour in. Those who could gave money and parcels of land, those who had less brought baskets of food.

In addition to Milo of Nogent, there was a rich man named Galo, and his wife, Adelaide, who presented the nuns with half rights in a mill at Crèvecoeur and some other property at Provins, along with sums of money. And before very long, the powerful overlord, Count Theobald of Champagne, came also to the assistance of the nuns.

Abelard wrote, as much to reassure himself as to establish the fact, that Heloise and her sisters received as much in one year from the friends of the Paraclete as he and his monks, had they remained, would have received in a lifetime.

"For inasmuch," he wrote, "as the feminine sex is feebler, so does their more wretched poverty more easily move the human heart, and their virtue is more pleasing to God as to man. And such grace in the eyes of men did the Lord bestow on our sister, who was over the rest, that the bishops loved her as a daughter, the abbots as a sister, the laity as a mother; and all alike marveled at her piety, her prudence, and in all things the incomparable meekness of her patience."

Abelard also mentions that during this time, Heloise kept herself out of sight and remained for long hours in her own cell that she might devote herself to meditation and prayer. When one considers the amount of work that had to be done to insure mere survival in that primitive place, one wonders how Heloise managed to spend those long hours in meditation. And yet, without them she might not have found the strength for all the work she had to do.

Now that Abelard had deprived her of his sustaining help, she turned to God, asking him for the strength to take upon her own shoulders a responsibility that seemed to require more moral and physical strength than she felt equal to alone.

The message which Paul sent to the Ephesians may well have been the answer to her prayers then and in the years to come: "Be strong in the Lord, and in the power of His might. Put on the whole armor of God, that ye may be able to stand against the wiles of the devil. For we wrestle not against flesh and blood, but against principalities, against the rulers of the darkness of this world, against spiritual wickedness in high places. Wherefore take unto you the whole armor of God, that ye may be able to withstand in the evil day, and having done all, to stand."

Was it not by taking such a stand that, in the year 1131, Heloise received papal recognition of all the gifts of property pertaining to the Paraclete? It would seem, at least, one result of those hours spent in her cell, that she should take proper precautions to establish rights of possession, so that she and her nuns and those to follow would never again be left vulnerable to any stronger forces which might choose to prey upon the convent.

One version of the way this precautionary measure was taken by Heloise is that she learned that Pope Innocent II, who was seeking refuge for a time in France, had been visiting a number of churches and monasteries, and had now reached Auxerre. Taking advantage of the pope's proximity, she went to see him and managed to obtain from him a bull which was one of the many that established the extent of the Paraclete's property and marked its growth under her administration.

This first document, of which the original still exists among the archives of the library of Châlons-sur-Marne, assured Heloise and all who came after her, of full possession of the gifts which they had then and would forever after receive. What was more, it promised to punish any who sought to do harm to the convent or to the nuns themselves. The Paraclete, by this same Bull of Pope Innocent II, was to be designated as "the Oratory of the Holy Trinity," and as such was to be taken under the protection of the apostolic see, and was to pay a sum of money annually to the Lateran Palace.

On the other hand, Henry Adams, in his *Mont St. Michel and Chartres*, offers as proof of Abelard's return to favor in 1136, that he secured from the pope in that year a bull which gave the oratory he had built, the rank and title of Monastery of the Paraclete—a novelty in the church tradition, Adams says, so extraordinary or so "shocking" that it still astounds churchmen.

There is more reason to believe that Heloise, with her growing sense of responsibility and wisdom, had put on the whole armor of God and had found a way to secure the Paraclete, her own fortress now, from the ravening wolves. It was up to her, as head of this growing religious community, to establish it upon a rock. Circumstances had forced her to be practical, a quality which was not difficult for her, as a Frenchwoman, to attain. Whether the responsibility had come to her from her own choice or not was no longer of any importance. It existed, and therefore Heloise became not only a good businesswoman, but, as she would have had to be in those times, a politician too.

And so, deserted as it would appear, once again by Abelard, she ran her convent wisely, learning how best to present her needs to those powerful and rich enough to meet them, and, having received the necessary gifts of money and land, how best to handle and preserve them.

She took no credit to herself. She was occupied now in the Lord's work. And there was plenty of this to be done, for which she was grateful. It was better to be busy throughout the long days and nights than to have time for the worries about Abelard which would have been unendurable now that the silence had come between them again. What hope, what reason could she possibly have to hope, that she was ever to hear from him again?

Even so, she worked to make the Paraclete not only a sanctuary for those who wanted to dedicate themselves to God's work, not only a place where prayers for the whole human race were spoken or sung at certain hours of the day—but a haven for Abelard, to which he could come and be cared for and comforted when he was ready to return.

Perhaps the hard work and the prayers and the dedication had silenced the lament in her heart: "By night I sought him whom my soul loveth; I sought him but found him not." For the day of his return seemed to stretch out into eternity.

14

Although, according to his own account, Abelard's life at this time was filled only by the troubles he was having with the monks of St. Gildas and the dangers encountered from his enemies whenever he traveled abroad, there is evidence to show that he took part in the important affairs of state and church as well. In fact, he seems to have been almost as much a leader of popular opinion as Bernard of Clairvaux himself.

For example, in February of 1130, when a schism broke out in Rome after the death of the pope, the cardinals elected two popes, one of whom was Innocent II. They appealed to France for help, and the heads of the French church agreed to support Innocent. The French king called a council, to be held at Etampes, for the purpose of declaring the loyalty of France to Innocent II. At this council were present Bernard of Clairvaux, Peter the Venerable of Cluny, and "the abbot of St. Gildas-de-Rhuys," who was none other than Abelard.

Furthermore, when, on January 20, 1131, Pope Innocent visited the Benedictine abbey of Morigny, the chronicles of the monastery record that among those present, in addition to the abbots of Morigny, Faversham and St. Lucien of Beauvais, were "Bernard of Clairvaux, the most famous pulpit orator of France, and Peter Abelard, abbot of St. Gildas, also a monk and the most eminent master of the schools to which scholars of almost all Latin races flowed."

In spite of this evidence, Abelard, writing his *Historia Cala-*

mitatum, lists only his troubles and none of his triumphs. If, as he has said, this long letter was written for the purpose of comforting a friend by showing him trials greater than his own, it is perhaps understandable that he dwelt on the evil that had befallen him rather than the good—although it has never been proved that anyone, even Job, was comforted by listening to a long account of another's tribulations.

Henry Adams has suggested that Abelard wrote the *Historia Calamitatum* at a period when he was feeling the shock of the brutal murder of the prior of St. Victor, which occurred a few miles beyond the walls of Paris, in August, 1133, and that this might have accounted for Abelard's constant fear for his life.

At any rate, we know from Abelard's account that, after establishing Heloise at the Paraclete, and being unable to remain there any length of time because of the criticism his visits had aroused, he returned to his monastery, St. Gildas, where he found conditions even worse than before.

He expelled the worst offenders among the monks, but this seemed to have no effect on the others. He appealed to the pope, who sent a special legate to enforce order. But even after this the monks were more disobedient than ever, and Abelard confessed that he was now not only in fear of being poisoned, but felt a dagger at his breast whenever he turned around. "In the very sacrifice of the altar," he wrote, "they endeavored to destroy me by putting poison in the chalice."

One day when Abelard had gone to Nantes to visit the count who was sick, and while he was in the count's house, some of his monks managed to put poison in a dish that was being prepared for Abelard's consumption. By "divine intervention," Abelard wrote, he refused the dish when it was offered, and it was passed along to one of the brothers who had accompanied him. Whereupon the poor monk who had innocently accepted and eaten the food fell down dead, and the servant who had prepared it fled.

And so, as Abelard took pains to record, thenceforth he openly avoided their traps as far as possible. He withdrew from the

congregation of the abbey and lived in a cell with a few brothers
whom he trusted. But each time he set out on a journey, he
declared, the wicked monks whom he had abandoned in anger
hired robbers and assassins to waylay him on the road in an
attempt to murder him.

Whether or not these fears were justified, one cannot but be
moved at these passages in Abelard's story. When one considers
his former fearlessness, and the brilliance of his mind, which
helped give clarity to the entire thought of the Middle Ages—
the Abelard who lectured to his students on the place of logic in
philosophy, who gave them Aristotle by way of Boethius, and
who explained the problems of universals—it is impossible not
to be saddened by this image Abelard himself gives of a badly
frightened man who saw threats and enemies lurking in every
shadow. For surely, to one as proud as Abelard, the belief that
he now was so much hated, when once he had been so much
loved, was unbearable enough—without the constant fear of
being poisoned or stabbed through the heart.

Along with the complaint that he lived in constant fear of the
enemies within and outside his own monastery, Abelard recalls
the legend of the tyrant Dionysius and of his subject, Damocles,
who believed that happiness depended on power and material
treasures—until he noticed the sword that hung over him by a
thread and so learned what happiness follows earthly power.

If he was seeking a moral with which to end his long jeremiad,
and trying to convince a friend of the insecurity that lay in
temporal power, no doubt he succeeded. Many of the miseries
Abelard described did occur after he was raised from ordinary
monkhood to the role of abbot of St. Gildas, which, though
remote, was traditionally the oldest abbey in Brittany.

But the *Historia Calamitatum* covered Abelard's whole life
thus far, that is, the first fifty-three or four years. And, as he
himself realized, there were many other causes for his suffering
besides the vindictiveness of the monks he tried to direct and
reform.

He closes this letter to "his dearly beloved brother in Christ

. . . and most familiar friend" with selections from the Old and the New Testaments.

"If they have persecuted me," he quotes from John, "they will persecute you. If the world hate you, ye know that it hated me before it hated you. If ye were of the world, the world would love his own."

And from Paul's message to the Galatians he cites: "I do not seek to please men. For if I pleased men, I should not be a servant of Christ."

Abelard brings the *Historia* to a close with the following: "Encouraged by these precepts, let us endure those things that befall us with greater confidence. . . . And as all things are governed by divine law, let each be comforted in his direst straits by knowing that God permits nothing to happen excessively, and that whatever happens adversely, He brings to a right conclusion.

"Wherefore let us say in all circumstances, 'Thy will be done.' What comfort there is for us in the words of the Apostle: 'We know that all things work together for good to them that love God.' And, in Proverbs: 'There shall no evil happen to the just.'

"Wherefore it is shown that those depart from the truth who are angered by an oppression of themselves, believing it to be directed against them by Divine Will, saying 'Thy will be done' and yet placing their own will before the Will of God. Farewell."

One of the many theories on why Abelard wrote the *Historia* is that it was a rather deliberately disguised plea to church authorities to release him from the restraints put upon him as abbot of St. Gildas, so that he would be permitted to throw off that burden and resume his lectures as a lay teacher. This was where his talents lay and what he longed to do.

If this is so, then Abelard was, in a way, justified. There is a document written by John of Salisbury, telling of his arrival in Paris as a student in 1136, and of finding Abelard teaching at Mount Ste. Genevieve, an independent school established outside the walls of Paris, but under the license of the bishop of Paris.

John of Salisbury, who became Bishop of Chartres in 1176,

and whose writings have formed a part of English Literature, went on to say, "I attached myself to the Palatine Peripatician who then presided on the hill of Ste. Genevieve, the illustrious doctor, admired by all. There, at his feet, I received the first elements of the dialectic art, and according to the measure of my poor understanding I received with all the avidity of my soul everything that came from his mouth."

If this were so, and there is no reason to doubt John of Salisbury, who exhibited in his writings not only a highly cultivated intelligence but a knowledge of practical affairs, then Abelard was holding classes outside of Paris with the permission of his superiors in the church, showing a return to favor.

There is also a more obvious reason why Abelard should have written that lengthy epistle. He was, above many things, a man of letters. His whole aim in life so far was to communicate his thoughts, his ideas, to others. Was it not only natural that, during that time of enforced residence in a cold, bleak monastery in the starkest part of Brittany, surrounded by evil and inferior minds, he should have resorted to a method of conveying his thoughts in writing to those beyond the monastery walls, to minds more attuned to receive his message than those within the range of his voice?

The practice of writing autobiographies was not as common in the twelfth century as it is today. In fact, with the exception of Saint Augustine's *Confessions*, there were almost no examples. Abelard, with a need to unburden himself in words, chose the form of a letter to a supposed friend, in order that the tension and wretchedness of his days would not drive him completely insane.

Some have said that the *Historia Calamitatum* was written with the hope that it would fall into the hands of Heloise. But there is no reason why, in that case, the letter should not have been addressed to her. That it did eventually fall into her hands, we know. But we are never told exactly how it happened, although she mentions receiving it "from a passing friend."

As unknown as is this friend of Heloise who delivered the

letter, or a copy of it, into her hands is the "friend" to whom Abelard addressed it. Surely the fame of being selected by Abelard as the recipient of his full confessions would have clung to any individual so honored. Yet not once is any actual person named, either by Abelard or Heloise or any of the later scholars who have had access to twelfth-century archives.

However the writing of this document relieved Abelard, and whatever the reasons for it having been written, what were the emotions of Heloise when she first read the *Historia Calamitatum?*

The joy of seeing his handwriting with her own eyes, at having news of him at last, was certainly outbalanced by the anxiety for his safety which the contents gave her.

Not only did the account of the constant attempts on his life distress her, but what must she have felt when she read Abelard's version of their meeting and their passionate affair? This part surely could not have been written with the thought that it would be read by her who had shared the love he so baldly described as lust!

However successful her efforts were over the long years to submit herself to God's will and to the church, the reading of that astounding epistle reopened old wounds, and caused her to live again all the joy, the pain, and the horror of their past together.

In spite of the vows and the intentions, the reading of that epistle brought back sharply into focus—if she had ever really been able to forget it—the fact that Abelard belonged to her, and she to him, forever, that nothing, not even his own cold account of what had passed between them, could kill the love she still bore him. Not distance nor convent walls, not even the divine law, which is called the will of God, could sever such a love.

How was he faring now, since the account of his trials was written? Was he still in danger? What of his present thoughts, his health, his state of mind? Where was he living, if he had succeeded in quitting the monastery of St. Gildas? What of a thousand little things concerning him that she felt she had to know.

Heloise shut herself in her cell to think—to pray and ask for wisdom of One who knew her best—and then she proceeded to pour out her heart to Abelard in one of the most beautiful love letters ever written.

*"To her master, nay father, to her husband,
nay brother; his handmaiden, nay daughter,
his wife, nay sister: to Abelard, Heloise*

15

"Your letter, my beloved, written to a friend for his consolation, has, by chance, just recently fallen into my hands. Seeing
at once that you, who are so dear to me, were the writer, I read
it eagerly that I might feel closer by your words, since I had
lost the real you.

"Alas! every word that I read was filled with gall and wormwood, that is, all that told the miserable story of our conversion and the long list of your unceasing suffering. How well
did you fulfill the promise to your friend, that in comparison
with yours, his troubles should seem lighter than air. Having
first described the early persecutions at the hand of your masters, and then the supreme treachery of the attack on your
body by my uncle, you told of the hateful jealousy of your fellow students, Alberic of Rheims and Lotolphus of Lombardy,
by whose instigation your incomparable treatise on the Trinity
was condemned to be burned and you, yourself, thrown
into confinement. From this you go on to tell of the
machinations of the abbot of St. Denis and the calumnies of
those false apostles, Norbert and Bernard, whom envy had
roused against you. It was even, you say, charged as a crime
against you for having given the name of Paraclete, the Comforter, to the oratory you had erected. And, finally, you tell
of the unceasing persecutions you have had to suffer from
those execrable monks of St. Gildas whom yet you call your
children, and to whose venomous conduct you are even, at
this moment, exposed.

"Who, think you, could read or hear these things and not be moved to tears? What then must have been my emotion, since the precise manner in which each event was described, caused me to renew my own sorrows, and not only that, increased my fears for your safety, since I perceived that the tide of danger was still rising against you. Are we then to despair of your life? And must our breasts, trembling at every sound, be made to wait hourly for news that may tell us you have been murdered!

"For Christ's sake, Abelard my beloved, (and He, I trust, as yet protects you) do inform us, His humble handmaidens, and thine, of the circumstances of your present dangers. I and my sisters remain, at least, of all your friends. Let us partake of your joys and sorrows. The sympathy of others brings some relief to the one who suffers, and a load that is laid on many shoulders is more easily carried. But should the storm subside a little, let us know of that, too, for your letters will be carriers of joy. In short, whatever may be their contents, to us they will always bring comfort, if only because they tell us that, at least, we are remembered by you. . . . I pray you, delay not out of negligence.

"No doubt it was to console your friend that you did write so long a letter. But by telling so faithfully of your own troubles in order to comfort him, you have greatly added to our desolation; in your desire to heal his wounds, you have inflicted fresh wounds on us, and enlarged those we had before. Heal, I beseech you, the wounds you yourself have caused, who are at such pains to heal those caused by and to others.

"You have answered the wish of your friend and comrade, and discharged the debt of both friendship and fellowship; but you are bound by a greater debt to us, who have been the most devoted of friends, and more than friends, daughters—unless a sweeter and holier name can be conceived.

"As to the greatness of the debt by which you are bound to them, there is no lack of proof, if proof were needed. For are you not, after God, the founder of this place, the builder of this oratory and the creator of this congregation? All that is here was begun by you. Nothing here was built on a foundation laid by others. This solitude had known no other men before you, no other dwelling before yours. In this wilderness of wild beasts and brigands, where the very name of God was not yet mentioned, you built a temple and dedicated it to the Holy Spirit. To build it you did not call upon the riches of princes or kings, although you could have called upon them. Instead, whatever was done was done by you alone. The clerks and scholars who flocked here, eager for your teaching, furnished whatever was needed, and even those who lived by ecclesiastical benefits—those whose wont it was to receive but not to give—in this place became most generous in bestowing gifts.

"But this new plantation dedicated to God is peculiarly yours, still. It is filled now with plants that are exceedingly tender and must be carefully watered if they are to grow. Even if it were not new, it would be weak merely through its feminine nature. . . . But you are tending an alien vineyard with admonitions that are often fruitless and holy sermons spoken in vain, while the vines you have not planted have turned bitter. You who spend so much care upon another's vineyard, think what you owe to your own. You teach and admonish ingrates and gain nothing. In vain have you scattered pearls of divine eloquence before swine. You who are so generous with the unruly, think what you owe to the obedient. You who give so lavishly to your enemies, considers what you owe to your daughters. And, even leaving out the others, then think what a great debt binds you to me, and perhaps what you owe to those women who are consecrated to God, you may pay more zealously to her who is yours alone.

"The holy Fathers wrote many serious treatises on the teaching and advice, and for the comfort of holy women. It is therefore amazing, that, after the tender beginning of our conversion, neither through reverence for God, nor by the examples of the holy Fathers, nor for love of us, have you ever attempted to comfort me, as I hesitate, and am already crushed by prolonged grief, either by speech in thy presence or by a letter in thy absence. And yet you know yourself to be bound to me by a debt so much the greater because you are tied to me by the sacrament of marriage, and even more than that, because, as everyone knows, I embraced you with an unbounded love.

"Thou knowest, my beloved, all men know it, what I have lost in thee, and how that infamous act which deprived me of you even tore me from myself. And that my grief is infinitely greater because of the manner in which I lost thee than from the loss itself. My Abelard, it is you alone who can help me now. By you was I wounded and by you I must be healed. It is in your power, alone, to give me pain, to give me joy, to give me comfort. And it is you alone who owe this to me. For this reason above all, that I have performed all things that you did order, even, because I could not refuse you anything, to the sacrifice of myself. My love for you had turned, in truth, to such madness that what I wanted most I cast away without hope of recovering, and, obeying your command, I changed my habit, against my heart, that I might show you to be possessor of my body and my soul. Nothing have I ever, God knows, required of you save yourself. Not for the vows of marriage, nor for any dowry, did I seek, nor my own passions or wishes, but thine only, as you well know, was I eager to gratify.

"And if to some the name of wife appears more sacred and more imposing, sweeter to me is the word friend, or concubine. The more I humbled myself to you, the greater right I thought to have in your favor, and the less harm I should commit against the fame you had acquired.

"And of this you were not unmindful, beloved, in the letter of which I have spoken, written to a friend for his comfort. In it you set forth the various reasons by which I tried to dissuade you from marrying me because we had shared our ill-starred bed. But you did not mention the many reasons I gave in which I preferred love to marriage, freedom to chains.

"I now call God to witness that if the Emperor Augustus,

ruler of the whole world, were to ask me to marry him that I
might rule with him over all, dearer would it be to me, and
far more precious, to be called thy mistress, or, if it shame you
not, your whore, than his empress.

"The fact that a man is rich and powerful does not make
him any worthier; those are the gifts of fortune, not of virtue.
And whoever would marry a rich man sooner than poor man,
desiring more in her husband than himself, is venal, and little
better than a prostitute. As Aeschines (he who was the friend
of Socrates) so clearly convinces us in his account of the conversation between Aspasia and Xenophon when she sought
to reconcile him to his wife: 'When you have understood this,
that in all the world there exists no better man or happier
woman, then you will seek that which is best above all things
—you to be the husband of so excellent a wife, and she to be
married to so excellent a husband.' Surely, a noble sentiment.
But that happiness which in other women could be the result
of fancy, in me is the truth. Since what they only believe of
their husbands, not only I, but the whole world knows to be
true of you.

"For who among emperors or scholars was your equal in
fame? What town or village did not clamor for a sight of you?
What wife or maiden did not long for you in your absence,
nor turn to fire in your presence? What queen or great lady
did not envy me my happiness and the bed I shared with you?
There were two qualities, among others, you possessed that
made you win all female hearts: the arts of making songs and
of singing them. What other philosopher possessed these gifts?
To ease the stern labors of the intellect, you composed so
many sonnets and songs on love that, the words and melodies
oft repeated by even the illiterate, have kept your name alive
to lovers in many lands. It was this, in part, that made so
many women envy me, through jealousy, then. For what
beauty of mind and body did not adorn your youth? What
woman who did envy me then does not pity me now, deprived of these delights? What man or woman, whether

formerly an enemy of mine or not, is not melted now by compassion for my lot?

"You know, my beloved, more than anyone, that, although I was the cause of your misfortunes, in spite of my guilt, I was, in truth, innocent. For it is not the deed that makes the crime, but the intention. Justice must weigh the intention by which we act, and not the act itself. What my reasons were for all my deeds none knows better than Abelard! I am ready to yield to your testimony. I call no other witness.

"Tell me one thing only, if you can, why, after our conversion, which you alone decided, I have been reduced to neglect and oblivion? Why, for all this time, I am never to be refreshed by your words of encouragement, nor comforted in your absence by your letters? Tell me, I beg of you, if you can—or rather, let me tell you what I feel and what others suspect! that it was sexual desire alone that joined you to me, rather than love. And when desire within you ceased, everything else was gone.

"This, my Abelard, my most beloved, is not only my opinion, but the opinion of all, not private but public. Would that it were peculiar to me and that others could find excuses and comfort me with them. Would that I could, by excusing you, find reasons to discover myself less vile than you would make me seem.

"Give your attention, I beg of you, to this small request of mine which should be easy for you to grant. While I am robbed of your presence, at least by written words, of which you have shown such an abundance, make me a gift of the sweetness of your mind that I may construct your image for myself.

"Up to now I have believed that I have deserved at least this much from you for whom I have done all things in obedience, even as a girl, when I took on the austerity of religious devotion not by my own vocation, but by your command, only. If for this I have earned nothing from you, then you may judge it all to have been in vain. For no reward may I expect from God, for love of Whom I have done nothing.

When you hastened to Him, I followed you, nay at your command, I went first. If, as I then may have thought, this was done because you had little faith in me, I grieved and was ashamed. For you should have known that I would, without hesitation, have preceded or followed you to the gates of hell, according to your word.

"For my heart was never with me, but with you. And now, more than ever, if it is not with you, then it is nowhere. For without you it cannot exist. I ask only what is good for you, and how can it not be well for you to give love for love, little for much, and words for acts? Sometimes I wish that your love, my dearest, had less trust in me and were a little more anxious! If I have made you confident in the past, let that not be cause for your neglect now. Remember, I beg of you, what I have done, and what you owe me. Many have thought that what I did with thee was for carnal pleasure only, or else, were uncertain whether it was from love or lust. But now, surely, they must know in what spirit I gave myself to you. I have denied myself all earthly pleasures that I might obey your will. I have kept nothing for myself, only this, to be now and always, entirely yours. Consider how unjust it is on your part if you give less to me who deserve more, when all that is demanded of you you could so easily give.

"By God, then, to whom you have dedicated your life, I ask you to give only so much of yourself as is at your disposal: that is, to send me some words of comfort, so, my mind being more at ease, I may serve Him more willingly. When, in former times, you looked to me for pleasure, how often did I hear from you! By your songs the name of Heloise was on every tongue, it was heard in every street, the walls of every house echoed it. How much more suitable that now your words should call me to God, whose words once excited me to desire. Consider all this, I beg you. Think on my petition.

"And now, although my letter has been long, my conclusion will be brief. *Farewell, my all.*"

16

Whatever answer Heloise expected from this passionate appeal to Abelard for a sign that he still loved her, his reply froze her hopes. The very manner in which he addressed her prepared her for the contents: *"To Heloise his dearly beloved sister in Christ, Abelard her brother in the same."*

He gave as his excuse for not writing to her that so great was his belief in her wisdom and ability to manage her own affairs, and those of the nuns in her charge, that he had not considered she would need his advice or comfort. From the whole tone of his letter, it is obvious that his intention was to turn her thoughts away from him as her husband by reminding her that she was now, in truth, the bride of Christ and none other.

Disappointing as this was to Heloise, she was too sensible a woman to have dreamed that his response would be otherwise. Abelard had changed, if she had not. The ardent lover she remembered, who had stopped at nothing to make her his own, existed no longer. To remind him of the man he had once been was unconscious cruelty on her part. He had been compelled to adjust himself, crippled as he was in a physical sense, to a life which permitted no emotion except that stirred up by the intellect. And what was more, if, as Heloise had declared so many times, she had no sense of sin in loving Abelard, he, on the other hand, who had been punished publicly for having loved her, was still doing penance and would continue atoning for his guilt until the day of his death.

He urged her to pray for him, and for this purpose he sent her a psalter, which he says she had asked for, though there is no evidence in her first letter that she made any such request. "Sister, once dear in the world, now dearest in Christ," he wrote, "with this psalter, for our great and many excesses, and for the daily perils in which we walk, may you offer up a perpetual sacrifice of prayers to the Lord."

He wrote of the value before God and the saints that the prayers of the faithful hold, especially the prayers of women for their loved ones, and of wives for their husbands. For several paragraphs he continues in this vein on the virtue of prayer, liberally sprinkling the pages with quotations from the Old and New Testaments and from the writings of the saints.

"What man has done amiss," he wrote, "the pleading of a woman has wiped clean." Therefore he asks her to consider how her prayers in his behalf might prevail before God. And, if she alone cannot succeed with her prayers in protecting him, then the convent of virgins and widows who are with her might succeed with their supplications for him. "For is it not written that 'where two or three are gathered together in My name, there am I in the midst of them,' and also 'If two of you shall agree on earth as touching anything that they shall ask, it shall be done for them of my Father which is in heaven.' Ye know, dearest sister, from the writings of St. Gregory, what aid the prayers of his brethren brought to an erring brother.

"And may that example induce you and the convent of holy sisters to prayer, that I may be kept alive for you through Whom, according to Paul, women have seen their dead restored to life. . . . and with but few intercessions were these resurrections accomplished. Indeed, many of those raised from the dead were not even of the faith, while with us not only the integrity of our faith but our profession of the same vows unites us.

"But now let us, forgetting for a moment the convent of women over which you preside, come to thee alone, whose great sanctity I have no doubt is effectual with the Lord, just as I do not doubt that thou art sworn to do all that is in your power for me above all men, especially when I am undergoing such great adversity. . . . Remember me always in your prayers who is especially thine! Listen, I beg of thee, with thine heart, to what thou hast so often heard with thine ear . . . and to those prayers which you and your convent used to offer up in my presence . . . now when I am absent, and in greater peril, add at the conclusion of each hour, this proper form of prayer:

"*Response:*   O Lord, Father and Ruler of all my life, leave me not to their counsels, and let me not fall by them.

Versicle: Take hold of shield and buckler, and stand up for my help. Leave me not.

Prayer: Save thy servant, O my God, whose hope is in Thee. Send him, Lord, help from Thy sanctuary, and watch over him from Sion. Be unto him, O Lord, a tower of strength from the face of his enemy. Hear my prayer, O Lord, and let my cry come unto Thee. (*Let us pray.*) God Who through Thy servant hast been pleased to gather Thy handmaids together in Thy name, we beseech Thee that Thou wilt protect him from all adversity and restore him in safety to Thy handmaids. Through our Lord, etc."

Then, having told Heloise exactly how she was to pray for him, Abelard instructs her still further by telling her what to do in case he is delivered into the hands of his enemies and slain by them. "I beseech you," he wrote, "wherever my body, either exposed or buried, may lie, have it brought to your cemetery. . . . for I think no place to be safer for a soul grieving for its sins and made desolate by transgression than that which is consecrated to the true Paraclete, the Comforter. . . . Nor can there be a fitter place for Christian burial among the faithful than among women devoted to Christ. For was it not women who, solicitous for the sepulcher of the Lord Jesus Christ, came to it bringing precious ointments, and went before and followed, diligently watching about His sepulcher and bewailing with tears the death of the Bridegroom, as it is written . . ."

"But this lastly above all things I demand of you," Abelard wrote, "that whereas now ye labor in too great solicitude for the welfare of my body, then being solicitous especially for the salvation of my soul ye show to the dead man how greatly ye loved the living, to wit by your special prayers.

"*Live, prosper, and thy sisters with thee.*
Live, but in Christ be mindful, pray, of me."

So Abelard ended this long awaited letter to Heloise.

What had she expected him to say? Who knows? She had asked him, had she not, to let her know how he was faring, whether well or ill. She had complained, not without bitterness, because he had written to another and not herself of his trials and tribulations. Why then should this first letter from Abelard, which she knew had caused him no little effort to write, have distressed her so much that her response was like a cry of anguish? Heloise, for all her intellectual attainments and for all her strength of character, never lets us forget how utterly feminine she was.

Although she had specifically asked Abelard for instruction in the way she should conduct her convent, appealing to him as the founder of the Paraclete and her superior in the church— the thing she so clearly wanted was a sign from her beloved, her husband, that what she had never ceased for a moment to feel toward him was in some measure reciprocated.

And what she received was a greeting from which all personal emotion had been carefully, scrupulously removed, fine words of praise for her virtues, and a meticulously prepared system of rules by which she and her convent of nuns were to pray for the soul of one in danger, not only of ordinary pitfalls, but of violent death. As an added boon, she was asked to prepare for his burial, as if it would console her to know that, though she could not have the joy of his presence in life, she would be assured of his body in death—that she and her sisters might pray over it.

Heloise had begged him for the bread of her life, and Abelard had replied with a stone. Her second letter was an even stronger appeal for sympathy and love. It began: "*To her all, after Christ, his all in Christ.*"

After a perfunctory paragraph in which Heloise merely ex-

presses surprise that Abelard should have placed her name ahead
of his in addressing his letter, she plunges into an expression of
the grief his letter has caused her.

"Whereas thou shouldst have given us comfort thou hast increased our desolation and caused tears to flow which thou
shouldst have dried. For who among us could hear with dry eyes
what thou hast put towards the end of thy letter: 'If the Lord
should deliver me into the hands of mine enemies . . . so they
might slay me,' and the rest?

"O, dearest, with what state of mind didst thou think that,
with what lips couldst thou endure to say it? Never may God so
forget His handmaids as to let them survive thee. Never may He
grant that life to us which is harder to bear than any kind of
death. It is for thee to celebrate our obsequies, for thee to commend our souls to God, and those whom thou hast gathered
together for God to send first to Him, that thou may be no
more disturbed by anxiety for them, and so much the more joy-
fully follow us the more assured thou be of our salvation. Spare,
I beseech thee, master, spare us words of this sort, whereby thou
makest wretched women more wretched, and take not from us
before our death that which is our life. . . .

"Thou askest us, my all, that by whatever fate . . . thou
mayest end this life, we shall have thy body brought to our
cemetery that we may pray over thee from our memory of thee
whom we have known. How could you think thy memory could
ever be lost to us or that there would be any time or place for
us to pray when our extreme grief would rob our sense of reason
and our tongue of speech? How should we speak to God when
our minds, grief-stricken through loss of thee, would anger Him
with our complaints? We should be more fit for burial with thee,
than to bury thee. . . . The very mention of thy death, my all,
is death to us!

"Spare us, therefore, I beg of you, at least spare her who is
thine alone, the use of words that pierce our souls. 'For to what
end,' said Seneca, 'anticipate evil, and before death lose one's
life?' Which also, well considering, the poet says to God:

May whatsoever Thou hast in store
Be swift and sudden. Let the human mind
To future destiny be ever blind
Allow our fears to hope.

"Though with thee lost what hope remains to me. What reason would I have to continue this pilgrimage save this that thou art still alive, all other pleasure from thee being forbidden me, even to enjoy your presence so that at times I might be restored to myself.

"O—if I dare to say so—cruel to me in all things God! O inclement clemency! O unfortunate fortune which has already spent the arrows of its strength against me so that it has none left to assail others, nor, if any were left, would there be any spot left in me to wound! One thing among so many wounds it feared, lest I end my torment by death.

"Most wretched of the wretched, unhappiest of the unhappy, I, who once was raised so high, being preferred by thee to all women, have fallen so low. . . . Whom among great and noble women did fortune ever set above or equal with me? Whom has it so cast down and crushed with grief? What glory did it give me in thee; what ruin has it brought me in thee! Which, that it might make me the most wretched of all women, first made me the happiest. . . .

"What injustice has justice played on us, that while we enjoyed the delights of love, abandoning ourselves to fornication as it is called, divine reproof was spared us. But when we corrected the unlawful state with the lawful, and covered the vileness of fornication with the sanctity of marriage, the weight of the Lord's hand fell upon us, nor did he allow an immaculate couch who had long endured one that was polluted.

"For what thou didst suffer would have been fitting punishment to men taken in most flagrant adultery. What they deserved thou didst incur by a marriage in which thou sought to make amends for all thy wrongdoing. What adultresses bring to their lovers thine own wife brought to thee. Not when we were indulging in our pleasure, but when, already separated for a time, we were living chastely, thou in thy school in Paris, and

I, at thy command, among the nuns of Argenteuil. When we were thus divided, that thou might more studiously devote thyself to thy school, and I the more freely to prayer and the meditation of holy books, while we were living then in greater holiness and chastity than before, thou alone didst pay the penalty in thy body for what we both alike had committed. Alone wert thou punished though both of us were at fault; and thou, the less guilty, hast borne all. For all that thou didst was to exalt me and all my race, so thou hadst given less cause for punishment both to God and to those traitors."

Once again we have proof that there was very little of the martyr in Heloise. Unlike some of her sisters in the church, she was first and forever a realist. No matter how deep her religious convictions may have been, or how superficial, she made all the protest of which she was capable against what seemed to her clearly a miscarriage of justice, whether God's or man's.

All the bitterness that she apparently had been storing up in her heart during those long years of meditation and prayer, when she should have been learning acceptance and humility, now appeared in this second letter to Abelard. Time had done nothing to dull the sharp edge of her pain. She was still outraged, not against blind fate but specifically against those who had brought harm to her beloved, namely her uncle and those others who had betrayed him.

And all the time that she was instructing the nuns under her and carrying out the rule of St. Benedict to the letter, Heloise kept two fires burning, one, her passion for her husband, and the other, her resentment that God, who represented justice as well as love, should have punished Abelard and herself not while they were engaged in what the law called sin, but after they had sanctified their love by marriage.

Overanxious to absolve Abelard of a sense of guilt, she took a large measure of the blame for their unhappiness upon herself. Was it not true that since Adam and Eve, woman had tempted man and brought him to grief? she argued. "She who had been created for him by the Lord as a helpmeet was turned to his supreme destruction."

She goes on with the examples of Delilah, who alone overcame the strong Nazarite, and of Job's wife, who urged him to curse God. "Thanks be to God," she adds, "for this at least, that the tempter did not draw me into guilt by my consent, like the women aforesaid, although he turned me, through my love for thee, into a cause of the wickness that was done."

"But even though innocence may purge my heart," Heloise wrote, "nor does consent involve me too heavily in guilt, yet many sins went before it which do not allow me to escape the blame. For long before, succumbing to the delights of carnal snares, I then deserved what I now bewail, and the sequel is made a fitting punishment of my former sins.

"Oh, that I may have the strength to do fit penance for this fault, especially that I may be able in some measure to recompense by the long contrition of penitence that punishment of the wound inflicted on thee, and what thou to the present hour hast borne . . . may I all my life long, as is right, take upon my mind, and in this way satisfy thee at least, if not God. For if I am truly to set forth the ills of my most wretched heart, I find no penance wherewith I may appease God Whom always for that outrage I charge with the utmost cruelty, and, therefore, offend Him rather by my indignation than appease Him by my repentance.

"*For what repentance of sins is that, however great the mortification of the body, when the mind still retains the same will to sin, and burns with its old desires?*"

So she wrote, whose life was spent in mortification of the flesh and in almost perpetual prayer for the redemption of the human race.

After quoting St. Gregory, who said, "Some there are who in open speech confess their faults, and yet in confession know not how to weep, and say lamentable things rejoicing," Heloise wrote: "So sweet to me were those delights of lovers which we enjoyed in common that they cannot either displease me nor hardly pass from memory. Nor even when I am asleep do they spare me their illusions. In the very solemnity of the mass, when prayer ought to be more pure, the obscure shades of those delights captivate my wretched soul and I pay heed to their vileness rather than to my prayers.

"And when I should lament for what I have done I sigh rather for what I have had to forego. Not only the things that we did, but the places also and the times in which we did them are so fixed with thee in my mind that in the same time and places I re-enact them all with thee, nor have I any rest from them in sleep. At times by the very motions of my body the thoughts of my mind are disclosed, nor can I restrain the utterance of unguarded words.

"Oh truly miserable I and most unworthy to utter that complaint of the stricken soul, 'Who shall deliver me from the body of this death?' And would that I might truthfully add, 'I thank God through Jesus Christ our Lord.' That grace, beloved, came to thee without your asking, and a single injury to thy body has cured many in thy soul, by which God by seeming to be more against thee, is found to be the kinder. Just as a faithful physician does not spare pain that he may show the way to health.

"But in me these thorns of the flesh serve only to stimulate the fervor of my youth. Those who say that I am chaste have not discovered the hypocrite in me. They make purity of the flesh a virtue, when it is a virtue not of the body but of the mind. . . . It is written, 'Depart from evil and do good.' But in vain is either done unless it be done in the love of God."

Then Heloise makes the statement which may have shocked Abelard even more than it has shocked those later readers who have had recourse to the manuscript in which it was written: "In my whole life, God knows, I have feared to offend thee rather than Him, and seek to please thee more than to please God. It was thy command that brought me to wear the garb of religion, not the love of God. See then how much more wretched I than all the others, since I endure all things here with no hope of reward in heaven."

She begs Abelard not to be deceived by her good behavior, or to mistake hypocrisy for religion, in commending himself to her prayers. Rather it is he who should pray for her! "Do not deem me healed, nor withdraw thy medicine," she asks. "Do not believe me to be not in want, nor delay to relieve my needs. Do not think me strong, lest I fall before thou hold up the falling." And she quotes: "*The heart is deceitful above all things, and desperately wicked: who can know it?*'"

She admonishes him to be fearful for her rather than to place so much trust in her, that she might be helped by his solicitude. "Now especially must thou fear, when no remedy is left in thee for my incontinence. . . . I seek not a crown of victory. It is enough to avoid danger. It is safer to avoid danger than to engage in battle. . . . In the words of St. Jerome, 'I confess my weakness, I wish not to fight in the hope of victory, lest, by chance, I lose the victory.' What need," she asks, in closing, "to abandon things certain, and to follow things uncertain?"

The poignancy of this cry touched Abelard. How could it have failed to do so? He knew Heloise better than any other human being ever knew her—the depth of her passion and her absolute honesty. Only the wildest and deepest love could have brought a woman to the utterance of such feeling as she expressed in this letter. Only a mind that hated deception and false prudery could have made such a confession.

Bound by the theology of her day, which held out a concrete heaven or hell as reward or punishment for one's conduct on earth, Heloise believed herself to be damned, not only in this life but for eternity. Yet she could not bring herself to lie about the true state of her heart.

"Thou shalt have no other gods before me," said a jealous Jehovah. But to Heloise, Abelard came before God, and she relinquished all claim to heaven rather than deny the truth.

17

From this distance in time there is no way to judge whether the love of Heloise for Abelard was greater and deeper than his for her. That he did love her is unquestionably true. When he was a young man he had loved her passionately and selfishly, but most young men in love for the first time are selfish. Later, however, in all fairness to him, it must be admitted that he protected her as far as he was able to do so. When she was bearing his child, he took her to his home in Brittany, knowing that she would be safe there and well taken care of by his sister. And after all, it was Abelard who insisted on marriage, in spite of all Heloise could do to convince him he would be ruining his promising and brilliant career. Furthermore, when he could do no more for her physically and materially, he arranged for her to be cared for spirtually and at the same time in such a manner that she would find safety and security for the rest of her life.

Abelard was a poet, a philosopher, and a great teacher. There was no simple path laid out for him to follow, as there would have been had he been a soldier, a farmer, or a nobleman occupied with the management of his serfs and his estates. And even beyond his thirtieth year he was a celibate who wrote romantic poetry and songs that inflamed others to commit the acts that he, as a fastidious youth, disdained.

When at last his own passions were aroused, he was unable or unwilling to control them. He found in the young and adoring Heloise a willing partner in those acts of love which he, in the aftermath of disgust with himself, called lust. And after the pain and humiliation of Fulbert's brutal attack, he had no difficulty in turning, with all his heart and soul, back to the pursuit of his original vocation, absorbing and dispensing knowledge.

That he was ever aware of a sense of responsibility for Heloise is evident enough in the fact that he provided a refuge for her and her little band of nuns at the Paraclete when they were driven from their convent of Argenteuil. Surely this was an act of love, however he may have explained it to the world. But how many men would have been so short-sighted as to consider that, having provided for her needs according to his own understanding of them, Heloise would then be content to go her own way in peace?

We know that Abelard was undergoing his own torments at this time, torments which he felt he had earned, but against which he nevertheless complained bitterly and volubly. In other words, he was sunk in his own wretched troubles, and felt that it was only natural that Heloise would devote her time to prayers for his safety, and not confuse him with her own troubles about which he could do nothing.

Her second letter to him came as a blow. Heloise, who was to be the rock on which his enfeebled frame could now lean, had brushed aside this trust in her with impatience and indignation. It was she, her letter stated in no uncertain terms, who needed still, and would always need, strength from him. He was not to endow her with such virtues as made things comfortable for him, but to consider her the frailest of vessels, a woman who needed her husband, who wished to be cherished and protected and shown the way, as much—and indeed much more—now that she was the abbess of her own convent as when she had stood with him before that secret altar and become his bride.

Abelard's reply to this letter, written after he had recovered from the shock, was slow and deliberate. He divided it into four parts, in each of which he attempted to follow her reasoning; to admonish and comfort her. He addressed it as follows: "*To the bride of Christ (from) the servant of the Same.*"

Thus he reminded her again, gently but sternly, that she was no longer the bride of Abelard, Pierre du Pallet, but of Christ Jesus alone. All through this lengthy epistle, one of the recurrent themes is that she must learn to turn her thoughts and her love away from him who was once her husband on earth and direct them solely to the Bridegroom in heaven whom she had pledged herself to love and serve forever more, deserting all others.

The letter began with some learned and rather pompous quotations from St. Augustine, St. Jerome, Vergil, and others. Then Abelard plunged into the heart of the matter. "It now remains," he wrote, "for us to take up that ever repeated complaint of yours, namely wherein you presume to accuse God for the manner of our conversion rather than seeming to glorify Him as is fitting."

He wrote that he had thought that this bitterness in her heart at so great an act of divine mercy would have long since disappeared—a bitterness which wore out soul and body alike, and was a source of misery and grief to him. If, as she had said, she wished to please him in all things, he begged her to lay aside this bitterness, "wherewith neither canst thou please me nor attain with me to blessedness."

He asked her not to grieve because his punishment was an act of injustice. "Had it befallen justly, wouldst thou have borne it more easily, or would it have offended thee less?" The consequences, he said, would have been worse for him, since it would have made his enemies praiseworthy and himself the more contemptible in the eyes of the world.

He reminded her that they had committed a sin even after they were married. After the pact of their marriage, he wrote, when she had retired to Argenteuil with the nuns in the cloister, he came to visit her there secretly, and "with the intemperance of his desire," as he called it, he made love to her in a certain part of the refectory.

"Thou knowest," he wrote, "how shamelessly we then acted in so hallowed a place, and one that was consecrated to the Most Holy Virgin. Which act, all other shameful acts apart, must be a token of a far more dire punishment."

He then went on to remind her of earlier "most shameful pollutions" which preceded their marriage, and of the manner in which he turned her uncle away from her and betrayed him. "Who would not consider that I was justly betrayed," Abelard asked, "by whom so shamelessly I myself had first betrayed."

Did she think, he asked, that the momentary pain of that wound he had received sufficed as punishment for those crimes which they had committed and which he had just recalled to her? In fact, he called that wound "most wholesome," and considered the real punishment which God had inflicted to be the wounds without ceasing which he now had to bear daily.

He reminded her, if she still had any doubts that they deserved to be punished, of the time when he carried her, pregnant, to his own country, of how she had put on the sacred habit and feigned to be a nun in order to escape from her uncle's house, and of how, by such pretense, she irreverently betrayed her religion. If she would think on these things, she would call what God had done to them not so much His justice as His grace.

"Take heed," Abelard wrote, "take heed, beloved, with what dragnets of His mercy the Lord has fished us up from this so perilous sea, and from the jaws of what a Charybdis He has saved our shipwrecked but unwilling souls, so that each of us may cry: 'Yet the Lord thinketh upon me.'"

He then asked Heloise to consider from what dangers the Lord had rescued them, "how wisely he made use of the evil that the most just injury to one part of my body might heal two souls"—and thus he went on, for page after page, to reveal with what loathing he now regarded those acts of concupiscence they had once enjoyed together. Not once did he seem to consider the wounds that his words might inflict on poor Heloise as she read them.

"Thou knowest," he reminded her, "to what infamy my inordinate lust had sacrificed us, until no reverence for honor, or even for God, could keep me from wallowing in that filth."

God had been good to him, he wrote, by removing that vilest member and cleansing him in a way that would aid the salvation of his soul and set him free for the honorable ministration of his office. "Truly," he wrote, "the Lord thinketh upon me. I will go and declare what the Lord hath done for my soul."

Then, after this expression of reverence and gratitude for having been saved from all that was sordid and vicious, Abelard remembered Heloise again, and murmured graciously enough, "Approach then also, my inseparable comrade, in a common thanksgiving. For the Lord is not unmindful of thy salvation. He, in His clemency, has resolved to aid two in one, which two the devil strove in one to extinguish."

For, Abelard said, the Lord had bound them by the "indissoluble law of the nuptial sacrament." When he, Abelard, had desired to retain her, who was beloved beyond measure, to himself forever, and had they not been thus bound in matrimony, on Abelard's withdrawal from the world, either by the suggestion of her kindred, or by her own carnal desires, she might have clung to the world.

Instead, it was if the Lord had reserved them for some great end, so that the talents of them both should be used for the glorification of His name.

Had she remained in the world, Abelard wrote, she might have brought forth a few children in pain. Instead, she had now borne many spiritual daughters for the Lord. She had, he reminded her, turned "the curse of Eve into the blessing of Mary." How much better it was that her holy hands should turn the pages of the sacred books than that they should serve the obscenities of womanly cares.

He urged her to think on Christ and to be like the women who were present at His sepulcher, those who bewailed and lamented and prepared ointments for his burial—"spiritual ointments, not corporeal." He told her to be compunctious over these duties with the whole force of her devotion.

"This lamentation, this wailing, be thine, sister," Abelard wrote, "who has given thyself in happy matrimony to the Bridegroom. He truly loved thee, and not I."

With what anguish Heloise must have read that line and those that followed. "My love," Abelard continued, "which involved each of us in sin, is to be called lust, not love. I satisfied my miserable desires in thee, and this was all that I loved. For thee, thou sayest, I have suffered, and that may be true, but it was rather through thee, and that against my will. Not from love of thee, but by compulsion of myself."

And then: "Weep for thy Savior, not for thy seducer; for thy Redeemer, not for thy defiler; for the Lord dead for thee, not the servant living who is for the first time freed from death."

Brutal as this letter was, Abelard's purpose was to deny Heloise even the smallest vestige of hope that they could ever be husband and wife again in the intimate sense as ordinary men and women. God had parted them for His own reasons which Abelard was beginning to understand, and which he wanted her to understand as well. Soft words would not have impressed her or have helped her as well as these bitter truths. It was necessary to wield a sharp knife, even if it had to be plunged directly into the heart of Heloise—just as God had inflicted pain on him in order to set him free.

Those visions which Heloise had confessed came to her in the midst of her duties had to be destroyed. There had to be nothing left to her of the past they had shared, not even memories, and Abelard had to be ruthless now to end forever that almost unbearably touching appeal for human love. Heloise had to be taught on which side she must cast her net—the right side, the church. On the other side, there was nothing for her at all.

Abelard's letter drew to a close with a prayer that he composed for Heloise, one that she and her nuns might repeat as suppliants to the Lord for him. "Thou hast joined us together, O Lord, and thou has put us asunder when it pleased Thee and in the manner that pleased Thee. Now, O Lord, what Thou hast mercifully begun most mercifully finish. And those whom Thou hast divided one from the other upon earth join to Thyself in heaven."

He ended the letter, "Farewell in Christ, bride of Christ. In Christ farewell, and in Christ dwell. Amen."

18

The next letter from Heloise to Abelard reveals to what extent she was subdued by his reproaches and instruction. What an effort it cost her to dam up her longings and appeals and expressions of love in order to submit to the command of Abelard that henceforth she regard him only as a brother in the service of the Lord. But the salutation of this letter is rather strange, considering her submission: *"To her Lord, (from one) who is specially his, uniquely."*

She then begins: "Lest thou shouldst find cause to blame me in anything for disobedience, I have set the bridle of thine injunction upon the words of my unbounded grief, that in writing, at least, I may moderate those expressions which in speech it is almost impossible to avoid. For nothing is less in our power than the heart, which we are forced to obey rather than to command. . . . accordingly is it written, 'Out of the abundance of the heart the mouth speaketh.' . . . I will hold back my hand therefore from writing what I cannot refrain my tongue from speaking. . . . Would that the heart . . . were as ready to obey as the hand of the writer."

She then makes two requests of Abelard: one, that he will instruct her on the origin of order of Benedictine nuns and on the authority for their profession; and the other, that he will institute some rule for her convent and set it forth in writing, definitely describing rules for the nuns that she professes not to have found in any of the writings of the holy fathers.

Since there already existed the *Regula Donati*, a rule for nuns composed in the middle of the seventh century, which embodied some portions of St. Benedict's *Regla*, and, since Heloise seems to have had access to most of the Latin texts then in existence, it would seem as if her request to Abelard was an easily understandable and forgivable device whereby she might hear from him again. If he considered that his last letter had settled everything between them, she could not bear to have this so. By making a request for instruction, not only for herself but for the nuns he had installed at the Paraclete, she was making sure that he would write to her again, which was all she could hope for now.

However, it is true that the rule of St. Benedict gave only general directions for many things and left numerous details to the discretion of the abbot. And, since everyday living and changing conditions kept bringing up new questions to be decided, Heloise was glad of assistance in making a correct choice in these matters, so that she might meet the spirit of the rule and follow the approved traditions.

There were specific things she wanted to know. Heloise was a realist, that is, she was practical and down to earth in spite of her highly developed romanticism and her intellectual attainments. She wanted to know, for instance, what her nuns were to wear, what they were to eat, "the state and habit of their conversation," as she put it, and other details which might apply specifically to the "feebler sex," since the holy fathers appeared to have neglected to observe that there was a difference between men and women.

"What," she asked, "is to be found in the rule of St. Benedict touching cowls, femorals and scapulars" which does not concern men alone? "How also does it touch us that the abbot himself should read the Gospel and thereafter intone a hymn? What of the abbot's table, set apart for him with the pilgrims and the guests? Is it becoming that an abbess should ever give hospitality to men, or that she should eat with those men whom she has taken in? Oh, how easy a step to the destruction of the souls of men and women is their dwelling together in one place! . . .

but especially at table where gluttony prevails and wine is drunk."

This last question was an important one, because the convents were under the supervision of the bishop in whose diocese they were located. And the bishop, who had the right to visit the convent to consecrate the abbess and the nuns, also had the right of "guesting," which meant that he could take up quarters for the night at the convent with an entire retinue, including horsemen, horses, and servants.

Even if the convent admitted only women to the hospitality of their table, had not St. Jerome exhorted nuns to shun the company of women of the world? What was more, Heloise said, if they admitted women only and excluded men from their hospitality, would it not offend the monks, whose services nuns required and from whom they received so much and appeared to bestow little or no gratitude in return?

Furthermore, Heloise wanted to know if it should be the custom for nuns to go out together to gather the harvest and undertake the work of the fields. This and numerous other problems had to be resolved for her, she said, for "What more presumptuous than to choose and profess a life of which one knew nothing, or to make a vow which could not be fulfilled?" Should not the strength of those upon whom burdens are imposed, be first considered? "Who lays such burdens upon an ass as he deems fitted for an elephant? Who demands the same from children and the aged as from men? That is, the same for the weak as for the strong, for the sick as for the well, for women as for men?"

As for the question of food, Heloise said, "We should be given a safer and milder indulgence, since nature has furnished us with greater virtue of sobriety. For it is evident that women can be maintained at a far more sparing cost and with less nourishment than men, nor does physic teach us that they are so easily inebriated."

And so she goes on for pages, liberally sprinkling them with quotations from the holy fathers and from the New and Old Testaments. It is as if she were trying her utmost to prove to her beloved that she had obeyed him and turned her mind solely toward her duties as abbess of the Paraclete. It was a desperate attempt to keep the correspondence between them alive, to force an answer, so that she might not lose him again to that awful silence. If he feared her ardor, and shrank from it with the repugnance of the resigned ascetic, very well, she would be dry as dust—just so long as he could be induced to write to her, for the contact of the written word was better than nothing.

But even so, there comes through these pages of questions and learned quotations some of the philosophy of Heloise, as if, in searching to find matter to interest Abelard, she had searched deep into her own mind and discovered what she believed, her own precepts and motives—now that she could no longer lean on his.

After she has asked him to give her rules for the feeding of her nuns, she says, "No great care need be given to those things which do not prepare us for the Kingdom of God, or which commend us least to God. . . . For the kingdom of God is not meat and drink, but righteousness and peace and joy . . . 'All things indeed are clean, but the evil is in the man who eateth to offend . . .' As Paul himself has said, writing to the Corinthians, 'But meat commendeth us not to God,' and to the Colossians, 'Let no man therefore judge you in meat or in drink.'"

She then goes on to ask why, if nuns are dead in Christ from the laws of the world, are they subject to such ordinances as "touch not; taste not; handle not," which are the commandments of men? For they owe men nothing, dwelling now not in the world. "Did not He, when he ordered His disciples to preach the gospel, although it was necessary to avoid all scandal, yet allow them the eating of all meats offered them by those who should hospitably invite them in, to wit, eating and drinking such things as might be set before them?"

And she quotes from Paul's epistle to Timothy: "Now the Spirit speaketh expressly, that in latter times some shall depart from the faith, giving heed to seducing spirits, and doctrines of devils; speaking lies in hypocrisy; forbidding to marry, and commanding to abstain from meats, which God hath created to be received with thanksgiving of them which believe and know the truth."

It is, she believed, more important to occupy oneself with the inner man, than with the outer: "By no outward thing is a man defiled, but from those things only which proceed out of the heart. Unless the spirit be first corrupted with evil intention, it cannot be a sin whatsoever is done outwardly in the body."

This recurrent theme, that it is the spirit or intention that counts more than the deed, was of the utmost importance to Heloise. If, as Epictetus said, everything has two handles, one by which it can be carried and one by which it cannot, then this theme was the handle by which Heloise could carry herself. No matter how grievous were the sins she had committed in the eyes of the world, she believed that the God who was love would understand and forgive.

Although her philosophy is implicit in what she writes in this letter, on the whole she manages to keep it impersonal, as Abelard had wished. She continues to ask him for rules whereby she may govern her convent, but asks him to be moderate in these, as befits the weak nature of women, and not to burden them with too many precepts, so that they might be free for the offices of divine praise.

She reminds him of the story of Mary and Martha: Mary who sat idle that she might hear the words of Christ, and Martha who toiled for Mary as well as for the Lord, and murmured as though in jealousy at her sister's repose. "Wherefore," Heloise said, "we see today those often murmur who labor in outward things when they minister earthly things to those who are occupied with divine offices . . . whereby it was by the sanction of the ministers of the church that the tribe of Levi should receive no earthly inheritance, but from the labor of others should take tithes and oblations."

She asks Abelard to advise her on the "abstinence of fasts," and also to give her provisions concerning the ecclesiastical offices and the order of the psalms. And, before everything else, she asks him to define what is to be done about the reading of the Gospel in the night watches. "For it seems perilous," she writes, "that at such times priests or deacons (by whom this reading might be intoned) should be admitted among us, whom it behooves to be segregated especially from every approach and from the sight of men; both that we may be able to devote ourselves more sincerely to God and also that we may be safer from temptation."

She ends the letter thus: "On thee now, Master, while thou livest, it falls to institute for us what is to be followed by us in perpetuity. For thou art, after God, the founder of this place. Thou, through God, art the planter of this congregation. Thou, with God, shalt be the institutor of our religion. A second preceptor after thee we may have, and one who shall build something upon another's foundation. And so, we fear, less solicitous for us, or less readily heard by us, and one who, although equally willing, may not be equally able.

"Speak thou to us and we will hear. *Farewell.*"

As far as we know, this was the last of the letters from Heloise to Abelard. The first of these was a great expression of a great love; the second was a cry of anguish, but in the third, Heloise showed great self-control. She restrained her emotions and wrote a letter that was impersonal from its beginning to the ending, with its brief *Vale.*

Whether or not Abelard's response was all that she hoped for, we do not know. But something that she had kept alive in her heart must have died at last, after a supreme struggle. When it was gone, there remained for Heloise only the present, and the future to be met with dignity.

Abelard's next two letters, written as if from a sense of duty, and in reply to her request for instruction, were as long as books and as scholarly. Heloise read them now without any fear of stirring up embers in the cold ashes that were left.

19

The first of these two letters from Abelard attempted to answer Heloise's question on the origin of nuns. Not wishing to disappoint her or to diminish her trust in his omniscience, Abelard obviously did a lot of research in the Old and New Testaments, as well as in the books of the great religious writers. The result was as much a tribute to dedicated women as it was an actual answer to her question.

There was, Abelard begins, an assembly of holy women with the mother of Jesus, who renounced the world and all their possessions to follow Christ. For many pages Abelard cites examples of these devout women: Mary Magdalene, Mary the mother of James, Mary the sister of Martha, and many others. He tells how these went in groups with the apostles, to minister to them as they had ministered to the Lord, and that in time these women "also possessed habitations of monasteries proper to themselves."

He refers to Philo, "a most learned Jew" who told of the church of Alexandria under Mark, describing consecrated places which were called *Senivor*, or monastery. With the men were women, among whom were virgins who had preserved the chastity of their bodies not from necessity but from devotion. These men and women established the custom of not tasting any food until sunset, and abstaining totally from wine. Their meat was bread and salt and hyssop, and their drink water. Among them none was either rich or poor, "that nothing be the property of any." Their patrimonies were divided among the needy, that they might devote themselves to prayer and psalms, to learning and to continence.

Abelard mentions that with these holy women, in addition to virgins there were many widows. Among examples of these, he gives the prophetess Anna, daughter of Phanuel of the tribe of Aser, who was of great age, "and had lived with an husband seven years from her virginity. . . . she departed not from the temple, but served God with fastings and prayer night and day."

With these examples, Abelard was encouraging Heloise, who was in a sense a widow, to do likewise. The rebellion he detected in her earlier letter caused him to fear that she might be tempted, and he wanted to convince her that, in her calling as handmaiden of the Lord, she was joined to a great sisterhood.

"Women," Abelard states, "were created in paradise, and therefore it becomes them most to pursue the celibate life of paradise."

Continuing to give further examples of women who had embraced chastity with such zeal "that they offered themselves in martyrdom to God, seeking to follow the Lamb, the Bridegroom of virgins," Abelard comes to the end of his letter.

If Heloise was sincere in her desire for information about the origin of nuns, then this was hardly an adequate answer to her question. On the other hand, there were sources available to her from which she could easily have found the answers.

Long before the year 300, when monasticism first made its appearance in Europe, the Institute of Virgins Consecrated to God, or "Brides of Christ," already existed. These women were highly esteemed by the faithful and occupied a place of honor at divine services.

At first they had no particular religious obligations. They adopted simplicity of dress and manners, and wore veils, like the married women of the time, as a protection against masculine advances. They also adopted a certain degree of poverty, charitable works, reading, seclusion and fasting. At first they made their vows privately, but after the third century, they made their vows before the bishop and the community, accompanied by consecration. They functioned under the bishops as assistants or helpers of the clergy.

Many of these women lived with their own families, but some of them selected a single cleric as a teacher and guardian, in return for which they kept house for him. This was called "subintroduction," and was sometimes a cause for scandal, so that eventually the bishops put a stop to it.

Others of the virgins grouped themselves in communities which were called "parthenons," from the Greek word meaning virgin. When St. Anthony withdrew from the world to lead a life of solitude, he entrusted his sister to one of these communities, or houses, of virgins.

Mary, sister of Pachomius, was the first nun, as Pachomius was the first monk to live in a monastery. He built a convent for her and her companions, in the year 330. During her lifetime there were at least 400 nuns in this convent at Tabennisi. Under the rule of Pachomius, a second convent was built, and then others, each having its own government. Life in the convents was similar to that of the monasteries. Each had a mother to rule the nuns. There were two important prayer hours, evening and morning. During the day the nuns learned to read and to write, memorized parts of the Holy Scriptures, notably the psalms, and observed days of fasting, and observed silence every day. Similar convents rose rapidly in Syria, Palestine, Egypt and Asia Minor.

In about the year 389, the Roman matron, Paula, founded three convents in Bethlehem. St. Jerome, who had influenced her, translated the rule of Pachomius for her use as a guide, but each of her convents had its own rule also.

In the year 410, St. Melania founded a convent in Jerusalem, on the Mount of Olives. And in 379, St. Basil founded a convent for his mother and sister which followed the rules he had established for his monks, but including the instructions that monks were to take over the spiritual directions of the nuns.

Toward the end of the fourth century, there were convents in many of the large cities of Europe. By their sermons, Ambrose, Jerome and Augustine were responsible for bringing a great many young women into these convents. Of these, St. Augustine was probably the most influential. His teachings laid stress on unity, love, humility and obedience. While he insisted that there be no personal property, he did not call for a uniform to be worn, merely suggesting that the nuns' clothing should not be showy, and that they should please by their conduct and not by their dress.

Augustine gave further suggestions. The nun's hair was not to be shorn, but to be covered with a net, over which a veil was to be placed, so that no hair showed. A bath was permitted once a month—except for the sick, who could have one more often, if necessary.

The nuns were not to be strictly enclosed but could appear in public. However, they were to conduct themselves with reserve. Each house was to have a mother at its head and she was to be assisted by a priest, to whom she was to pass on whatever was beyond her strength.

This rule of St. Augustine greatly influenced the growth of monasticism both for monks and nuns, and St. Benedict profited by it when he wrote his *Regla*.

The convents in France in Heloise's day closely followed the rule of St. Benedict. Surely, with this guide to instruct her, she could have run the Paraclete wisely and well, and in conformity with her sister convents.

Why did she then find it necessary to ask Abelard to give her a special rule, professing to find instances where the *Regla* was not enough to guide her? Was it to flatter Abelard? To let him know how greatly she still esteemed his instruction? Or to establish the fact of her spiritual need of him, since the physical need could bring no response except to alienate him further.

During those ten years at Argenteuil when she had been deprived of him so completely, Heloise had managed to get along, first as an ordinary nun, following instructions of her superiors, and then as a superior giving instruction to others. But now, having established a contact with Abelard, how could she bear to let him go again? It was only natural for her to use any means that were left to hold his interest.

She had reminded him that he was the founder of the Paraclete, and that therefore it was for him, and no other who might succeed him, to say how the convent, which bore the name he had given it, should be run.

And, as proof that Heloise understood the nature of Abelard better than any one else could know it, she had her wish. For, in spite of the personal difficulties Abelard was having at this time, he spent months preparing and writing the epistle, which is known as the eighth in their correspondence and which runs almost to book length.

It was a major undertaking, filled with classical and biblical references, revealing his extensive scholarship. But it also contained the rules that Heloise had asked for and that were without doubt, of great help to her.

Above all for Heloise, it was a sign of his interest. Why else would he have assumed so arduous a task? She was grateful for this sign, as she was for the rule. She had wanted something of Abelard's to keep with her for the lonely years ahead, and she had her wish. It must surely have been of some comfort, as well as a guide, on the long road she was to walk alone.

20

Thus Abelard began his long epistle, addressing not Heloise alone, but all of the nuns of the Paraclete of that time and the time to come.

The sum of the monastic system or religion, he points out in the first paragraph, is that one lives continently and without possessions in order that one may obey the teachings of Christ to the evangelists, which were to gird up their loins, forsake all that they had, and follow him.

Not only was this so for the disciples, but for those holy women and true nuns who also followed the Christ, and who were honored by Him and His disciples afterward. For woman is indeed holy, Abelard writes, when neither consent nor pride distorts her mind—not like the minds of the five foolish virgins, who beat upon the door which was already shut to them, crying, "Lord, Lord, open to us," and to whom the Bridegroom answered, "Verily, I say unto you, I know you not."

Naked we follow a naked Christ, Abelard declares, as the apostles did, forsaking not only our worldly possessions and the affections of our kin, but our own will, which we put behind us that we may live not according to our own judgment, but by the rule of our prelate who presides over us in the place of Christ. For what does it mean to deny ourselves unless we put behind us all carnal affections and our own will? He quotes Ecclesiastes: "Go not after thy lusts, but refrain thyself from thy appetites." For what else does it mean to bear the cross save to endure some torment?

When we wholly forsake those things which are ours we enter the apostolic life, which reduces all to a common store. As it was said, " 'And the multitude of them that believed were of one heart and soul. Neither said any of them ought of the things which he possessed as being his own, but they had all things in common.' " For it was divided each according to his need, otherwise they could not have lived without property, which consists rather in ambition than in possession.

Abelard then, after many pages on this same theme, goes into the admonition of silence for the nuns of the Paraclete. Because St. Benedict had said that at all times monks ought to study silence, Abelard says, "Let you at least subdue the tongue . . . in prayer, in the cloister, the dormitory, the refectory and in all eating and cooking; and from compline onwards let this be especially observed by all."

If necessary, Abelard said, let signs be used instead of words. And those words that must be said, let them be said briefly and let her who spoke them return quickly to her former duties or whatever is next to be done. And let these words be spoken in a place set apart for the purpose. For, as St. Gregory said, in the seventh book of *Morals*, "When we neglect to be careful of idle words, we arrive at harmful ones, those that sow incitement to quarrels, hatred and the loss of the whole peace of the heart."

According to Abelard, the Abbot Macharius in Syria told his brethren that after mass was said they should flee the churches. One of them asked where they should flee. Where could there be a greater solitude than in the church? And Macharius answered by putting his finger to his lips, saying: "There is where I say you are to flee."

For as Esaias the prophet said: "The work of righteousness shall be peace, and the effect of righteousness shall be quietness." Following these precepts, Abelard says, the Abbot Agatho held a stone in his mouth for three years, until he should learn to be quiet.

The place, Abelard pointed out, meaning the place of worship, does not bring salvation, but it furnishes a way of easier observance and for guarding it more safely. That is why, he says, the holy men of the Old Testament removed themselves to the wilderness and built huts for themselves along the River Jordan. John and his disciples, and thereafter Paul, Anthony, and Macharius, fled to the wilderness from the tumult of their times and from a tempting world, that they might devote themselves more earnestly to God. Christ Himself, when He wished to re-move Himself from the prompting of temptation, chose the secret places and avoided the noisy crowds. In this way, says Abelard, he consecrated for us the wilderness by the forty days of His fasting, withdrawing not only from the multitudes but even from His apostles. He plainly showed by this how greatly he valued the solitary places for us where we can devote our-selves more purely to Him.

As another example of the choice of solitude, Abelard cites the abbot Arsenius, who, while he was still living in a palace, prayed to the Lord to guide him to salvation. And a voice came to him advising him to flee from men and he would be saved. And after he had departed to the monastic life, Arsenius heard the same voice say: "Flee, be silent, be at peace. These are the roots of not sinning." Thereafter when anyone, even the arch-bishop, came to him for counsel, Arsenius sent him away.

And when one day a Roman matron visited Arsenius in his sanctuary, he said to her, "Why have you presumed to under-take this journey? Know you not that you are a woman and should never travel, or is it that you may return to Rome and tell the other women that you have seen Arsenius, and they will make the sea a road for women coming to me?"

The Roman matron excused herself and promised to advise other women not to come. But she asked him to pray for her and be mindful of her always. And he replied, "'I will pray God that He wipe the memory of thee from my heart." Later, when the abbot Mark asked why he fled from men, Arsenius answered, "God knows I love men, but with men and God equally I can-not be."

Then Abelard gives an example of one of the female sex who

sought solitude in as extreme a manner as those men he had mentioned. There was a virgin who refused a visit from St. Martin because it would interfere with her contemplation. She sent him a veil, and from her window called to him: "Stay where thou art, Father, for I have never been visited by a man." St. Martin blessed her and went his way, rejoicing and thanking God that he had met so chaste a woman.

What an insult would the bishops or prelates consider this repulse now, Abelard remarks. He then goes on to mention some of the abuses of the day, such as monks who dwelt in the wilderness building special houses for the entertainment of visitors from the world. Although many of the monasteries were originally established in the wilderness to avoid other men, the monks, after the first enthusiasm waned, deliberately invited others to join them for entertainment's sake, gathering men and maidservants around them to build and run great villages near their monasteries, "and thus," Abelard says, "have returned to the world, nay, have drawn the world after them."

He cautions Heloise not to follow such examples as these who have abused the rules. He reminds her pointedly of her "infirmity" which makes solitude the more necessary, so that she will be less likely to be attacked by the warfare of "carnal temptations." He quotes St. Anthony, who said: "He who dwells in solitude is snatched from the wars of hearing, speech and sight. And against one only shall he have to fight—the war of the heart."

One more reference is made by Abelard concerning the wisdom of seeking the desert and the wilderness as a dwelling place, and that is in the words of St. Jerome to the monk Heliodorus: "O desert rejoicing in the presence of God! What doest thou, brother, in the world, who art greater than the world?"

After advising Heloise on further structures for the Paraclete, such as a bakehouse with oven, and places where the sisters might perform their tasks so that there should be no need for them to leave the premises, Abelard turns to the way the convent should be governed.

Certain nuns are to be set over the others, with a single one in command, as in armies. This single commander, or superior, shall preside over the rest according to her judgment. For no congregation, Abelard says, nor any household for that matter, can remain entire unless unity is preserved by the magistracy of one person. "In a ship there is one steersman. In a house there is one master."

There should be appointed seven persons to carry out the administration of the convent. These were to be, namely, the porteress, the cellaress, the wardrober, the infirmarian, the chantress, the sacristan, and, lastly, the abbess. She should have the place of commander, the other six to be office-bearers. The rest of the nuns, the cloistral, were to perform the divine service after the manner of soldiers. The converts who have forsaken the world to dedicate themselves to the service of the nuns, were to wear a certain religious, but not monastic, habit, and to hold the lowest rank.

An abbess, Abelard said, (was he alluding to Heloise, or merely prescribing for those to come after her?) should be chosen for her age, or rather the maturity of her morals; because by obedience she has learned to govern, and because by work rather than hearsay, has learned the rule. Her selection should never be made from among noblewomen unless it is absolutely necessary, as "they are apt to be presumptuous or proud, especially when they are natives of the place in which the convent is located. As St. Jerome wrote to Heliodorus, 'A monk in his own country cannot be perfect. And not to wish for perfection is a sin.'"

By her example, the abbess should shine in all virtues, Abelard continues, lest by her own morals she contradicts those morals of which she preaches, and what she builds up by words, she destroys by deeds. Out of her mouth the word of reproval would be taken away if she were ashamed to correct others for the faults which she herself is known to have committed.

Like a watchful and careful captain, the abbess should go around her convent. Let her be the first to know of any evils that exist, so that she may correct them before they are known to others, let her understand that she has the custody of bodies as well as souls.

Next Abelard forbids the abbess to live more delicately than her sisters. She is not to have private chambers for eating, but she is to do all things with the subordinate nuns, so that she is with them constantly. It is true that St. Benedict, who was greatly concerned with pilgrims and strangers, set a table apart for the abbot to eat with them. But since his rule was established, it has proved best for the abbot not to withdraw in this manner, but to provide a faithful dispenser for the pilgrims. "For at table it is easy to fall, and then should discipline keep a stricter watch."

The abbess should not leave her convent, Abelard says, but if any mission to the outside is necessary, she should send someone else, preferably a monk. "For it behooves men to provide for the needs of women, and the greater the religion is, the more they devote themselves to God, the greater is their need for the assistance of men." For this reason there should be monks to provide for the nuns all those things that concern outward charges. Monks shall also be necessary for the masses, and for any work that is needed.

Regarding these monks who should look after the nuns' needs, Abelard goes on to say that they should be kept apart from the sisters, and have no permission to approach even to the vestibule of their private quarters, nor should they be permitted to converse with the abbess alone, but only in the presence of two or three nuns. Moreover, the conversations should be rare, the speech brief. "For God forbid," Abelard remarks, "that we should wish for the monks to be familiar with the virgins of Christ."

However, although the monks were to be kept separate and far apart from the convent, Abelard commits the sisters to their guidance, ordaining one monk, who has been proven, to have charge of the management of the convent's lands, the erection of buildings, and the performance of such chores as should leave the handmaids of Christ free for divine service.

Abelard then concerns himself with the special duties of each

of the seven nuns he has named, who are to carry on the administration of the convent.

The sacristan, who is also the treasurer, shall have charge of
the oratory, and shall have the keys to it. If there are any offer-
ings, she is to receive them. She is also to have charge of fashion-
ing or refashioning all the things that are needed in the oratory,
and its entire adornment. It is her duty to see to the hosts, the
vessels and books of the altar; the relics, the incense, the lights,
the clock, and the striking of bells. The virgins are to prepare
the hosts, having first purified the flour of which they are made,
and they are to wash the altar cloths. She who presides over the
sanctuary should be pre-eminently pure. She ought also to be
learned, especially in the computation of the moon, so that she
may provide for the oratory according to the order of the seasons.

The chantress shall provide for the whole choir, and shall arrange the divine offices, and have mastery in the teaching of
singing, reading and those things that pertain to writing or to
dictation. She shall keep a record of the books, giving them out
and receiving them, and shall take charge of the writing and
adorning of them. She shall arrange the seating of the choir, and
decide who is to read or sing, and shall compose the list to be
recited on Saturdays in the chapter, wherein the weekly duties
are described. It is therefore important that she be lettered and
have a knowledge of music. She also, after the abbess, shall see
to all the discipline.

The infirmarian shall take care of the sick, and preserve them
from sin as from want. She is to make allowances for whatever
the sickness demands, since there is a proverb that "the law was
not made for the sick." Meat is not to be denied the sick save
on the sixth day of the week or the chief vigils or the fasts of
the four seasons or of Lent. But it is important to keep them
from sin, since it is necessary for the sick to think of their departure from this world. Silence is to be observed, and they are
to be quick to prayer. There must always be a careful guardian
near the sick, who, should the need arise, may go quickly to
them. And there must be sufficient provision of medicine in
the house. Therefore, the infirmarian should be one who has a

knowledge of medicine, and it would be well if she had a knowledge of bleeding also, lest it be necessary to summon a man to enter among women for this purpose.

Provision must be made in the infirmary, for the offices of the hours, and for communion. As for annointing the sick, let there be brought in from among the monks one of the elder priests or deacons, bringing the sacred oil with him. Let the convent of sisters be present, yet with a partition between, as the sacrament is celebrated. Thus it is necessary that the sickroom be arranged so that the monks who are to administer communion may have easy access and egress, neither seeing the convent of nuns nor being seen by them.

And once each day let the abbess, with the cellaress, visit the sick. And if the sick person shall be near death, let the nun who is beside her run to the convent with a board, and beating upon it, announce her sister's departure to the whole convent that they may come quickly, no matter what the hour of day or night. And let whoever shall come running at the sound of the beating of the board, straightway begin the litany.

Then let the body of her that is dead be washed by the sisters, and after being clad in some cheap but clean garment, and in sandals, let it be laid on a bier, the head being wrapped in a veil. These garments are to be strongly stitched, or tied to the body, and are not to be removed afterward. The abbess shall have an honor above others only in that her body be wrapped in a shroud alone, and sewn up as in a sack.

The wardrober shall have charge of all that pertains to clothing, including shoes. She shall have the sheep shorn and receive the hides for sandals. She shall spin and store the flax or wool and have charge of the dormitory and provide beds for all. She shall have charge of table covering and of towels, and of the cutting, sewing, and washing of all cloths. She shall apportion her work to the sisters, and have charge of the novices.

The cellaress shall have charge of all that pertains to food, the cellar, the refectory, the kitchen, the mill, the bakehouse, the gardens and the orchards; of the cultivation of the fields, the raising of bees, also the herds, and flocks and poultry. She is not to be a miser, for "God loveth a cheerful giver." She shall, of course, not be more generous to herself in the distribution of food than she is to others, nor is she to provide special dishes for herself.

The porteress shall have charge of the reception of guests, or any who come to the convent—the announcement of their presence, the conducting of them to their destination, and the appropriate hospitality. She should be of an age and mind to know how to receive and answer questions discreetly, and to determine who are to be taken in and who are not, and how they are to be received. Because she is in the vestibule of the Lord's house, she should be mild in speech, and gentle with those whom she keeps out.

Since she has occasion to see the poor more often than the others see them, she shall distribute food and clothing as it is needed. There shall be a lodge by the gate for her and her vicar, and as they are waiting, they shall not sit idle, but shall study in silence.

Her duty is not only to keep men out, but to keep out gossip and rumors that they may not be carried into the convent. As soon as there is a knock at the door or gate, she is to open it. Only women shall be allowed in. Men are to be directed to the monks. No man is to be admitted for any reason until the abbess is consulted in the matter. But to women the gate shall be opened at once. They shall then be made to wait in a cell until the abbess, or sisters whom she may send, come to them.

In the case, however, of poor women who require washing of their feet, it is for the abbess or one of the sisters to perform this act of hospitality. For in the *Lives of the Fathers* it is said: "The Savior girded himself with a towel and washed the feet of the disciples, ordering them to wash one another's feet."

"I was a stranger," the Lord said, "And ye took me in."

21

After this careful and detailed instruction on the duties of the seven sisters who were to help the Abbess Heloise run the Paraclete, Abelard then goes on to give advice on the adornment of the convent, and other problems.

There should be only necessary ornaments in the oratory, he says, and nothing superfluous. Everything should be clean, but nothing costly. There should be no silver or gold, except one or more silver chalices. There are to be no ornaments of silk, except the stoles or maniples. There are to be no carved figures in the oratory, but a wooden cross is to be hung over the altar, on which may be painted the image of the Savior, if they wished. But the altar must have no other ornament. One pair of bells should be sufficient. A vessel of holy water is to be set just outside the entrance to the oratory, that the nuns may bless themselves going in and coming out, after compline.

As soon as the bell is rung, each nun is to put aside whatever she is doing and hasten to the divine office, without running. And on entering the oratory, she is to say, "I will come into thy house in the multitude of thy holy mercy, and in thy fear will I worship toward thy holy temple."

No book is to be kept in the choir save what is necessary for the office that is to be sung. The psalms are to be said distinctly so as to be understood, and not so loud but that those with weak voices shall be heard. Nothing is to be said or sung that does not come from the authentic Scriptures, chiefly the

Old and the New Testament. Sermons or expositions are to be recited only at table or in the chapter.

At midnight, the nuns must rise for the nocturnal vigils, so it is best that they retire early. After the vigils they may return to the dormitory until the hour of morning lauds. If any of the night remains, it should be used for sleeping, but if any of the nuns feel a special need for meditation or for study, let them do so without disturbing the sleepers.

The morning hour is to be performed as soon as day breaks; on the sun's rising the bell should be rung. If it be summer, the nuns may return to the dormitory to sleep for a little while before prime. This morning sleep is to be granted from Easter until the autumnal equinox, when the night begins to be longer than the day.

On leaving the dormitory, the nuns may wash themselves, and then sit in the cloister reading or singing until the bell for prime is rung. After prime, they are to go into the chapter and seat themselves, and there a lesson of martyrology may be read, or some of the rule be expounded, and there may be some edifying discussion.

Abelard next takes up the subject of discipline. He uses as his authority St. Augustine, who asked what place is entirely free from sin. "For no matter how vigilant be the discipline of my house," he said, "I am a man and among men I dwell."

No monastery or house should be called disordered, Abelard says, merely because disorderly things are done there, but only if, after they have been done, they are not carefully corrected. Therefore, whoever has seen something in another that should be corrected, and does not report it, should be subjected to a greater punishment than she who has committed the error. None should delay to accuse, whether it be her own fault or another's. Let none, however, presume to judge or punish another nun without first reporting to the abbess. Thereafter, if a council is held, it shall be the privilege of any nun present to offer her opinion, but the decree of the abbess shall hold fast, "even if, which God forbid, she be mistaken and decide upon that course which is worst." For it is far better, Abelard believes, to do well than to do good. What matters more than what is done is the manner or spirit in which it is done. (How closely this coincided with Heloise's own conviction!)

"And so," Abelard continues, "superiors are to be obeyed in all things, however great the material harm, if no peril is apparent in the soul." It is, however, up to the superior to see that she orders well. As often as there is need of counsel, it should not be postponed, but the whole convent should be assembled at once.

Returning to the subject of the nuns' activities, Abelard directs that, on coming out from chapter, they should attend to their proper works, such as reading, singing, or handicrafts, until terce. After terce, the mass is to be said, for the celebration of which one of the monks should be appointed each week. If the company happens to be great, he should come with a deacon and a subdeacon who may minister to him what is necessary. The coming in and going out of these monks should be so arranged that they are in no way visible to the sisters. If the communion is to be made by the sisters, a priest of ripe age should be chosen, who may give them communion after the mass, the deacon and subdeacon having first withdrawn "to remove any occasion for temptation."

After mass, the nuns are to return to their respective tasks until sext. Then comes dinner, unless it is a time of fasting, in which case they must wait until none, even until vespers, if it be Lent. In the summer they may rest in the dormitory until none, and then work until vespers. After vespers they may eat or drink, and then, according to the season, go to collation. But on Saturday, before collation, they are to be made clean, "to wit by washing of the feet and of the hands." After collation they are to come directly to compline, and then to sleep.

In respect to clothing and food, Abelard, first quoting from the apostle who said, "And having food and raiment let us therefore be content," decides that necessary things should suffice, nothing superfluous is to be sought. And only that which can be bought cheaply or secured easily is to be given to the nuns.

"For the kingdom of God," Abelard reminds Heloise and her sisters, "is not meat and drink, but righteousness, peace, and joy." All things are pure, but it is evil for the man who eateth to offend, or to go against his own conscience. For all that we do against our conscience, and against that which we believe, is sin. Citing Paul again, he adds, "There is nothing unclean of itself," only what we esteem to be unclean—and which offends others. "Wherefore, if meat make my brother to offend, I will eat no flesh while the world standeth."

At this point in his instructions to Heloise on the way the Paraclete is to be run, Abelard seems to go off at a tangent, and writes about marriage and adultery and second marriages for women. He quotes Paul on the subject: "I say therefore to the unmarried and widows, it is good for them to abide even as I. But if they cannot contain, let them marry: for it is better to marry than to burn."

It is difficult to understand why these passages should be inserted in a section of his letter where Abelard is answering Heloise's questions about the use of meat and wine at the Paraclete. And yet, it is here that Abelard chooses to quote from St. Paul on the subject of women: "Let them marry often rather than fornicate once, that if they be prostituted to one they pay not the debts of carnal commerce to many."

It is passages such as the above that have led some scholars to believe that the letters were tampered with by the monks who copied them, or by the earliest translators. However, it must be remembered that Abelard wrote this lengthy epistle to Heloise at a time when he was under great strain and feared for his life. It is possible that his mind may have wandered a little. On the other hand, it could well be that the passionate outbursts in the first and second of Heloise's letters to him, may have caused him still to entertain the fear that she could succumb to some carnal temptation if it were presented to her. Surely he needed no longer to fear that Heloise might marry again. And yet, from time to time, something resembling that thought seems to arise, and Abelard again becomes the human lover, all the more jealous because there is nothing he can offer his wife but the

walls of the convent in the wilderness near Troyes—and a seem-
ingly endless stream of words. No matter how avidly Heloise
awaited those words, or how beautifully they were expressed, he
must have had moments of doubt that they could take the place
of that ugly thing he called lust. But words were his gift, and he
gave them freely to Heloise who had begged for them.

On the subject of wine, whether it should be drunk by the
nuns of the Paraclete or not, Abelard says that by the rules of
St. Pachomius, only those who were sick should have access to
wine and liquor. St. Benedict, he declares, allowed wine to his
monks only by dispensation, and that because he found it impossible to persuade them that it was not good for them.

What St. Benedict had to say on the subject in his *Regla* is as
follows:

"It is with some misgiving that we determine how much
others should eat or drink. Nevertheless, keeping in view the
needs of weaker brethren, we believe that a hemina (about
half a pint) of wine a day is sufficient for each. But those upon
whom God has bestowed the gift of abstinence should know
that they shall have a special reward.

"But, if the circumstance of the place, or the heat of summer,
require more, let the superior be free to grant it. Yet let him
always take care that neither surfeit nor drunkenness supervene.
We do, indeed, read that wine is no drink for monks; but since
nowadays monks cannot be persuaded of this, let us agree to
drink temperately and not to satiety: for wine maketh even the
wise to fall away.

"But when the circumstances of the place are such that the
aforesaid measure cannot be had, but much less or even none
at all, then let the monks who dwell there bless God and not
murmur. Above all things do we give this admonition, that they
abstain from murmuring." ("*Hoc ante omnia admonentes, ut
absque murmurationibus sint.*")

Heloise must have read this rule of St. Benedict, but what she
specifically wanted Abelard to tell her was how it should be
applied to her convent of nuns.

He answers in rather a roundabout manner, quoting many

sources, but ends by saying, "Let women either abstain altogether in God's name, as the wives of the gentiles are forbidden wine from fear of adultery; or so temper their wine with water that it might satisfy their thirst and their health, yet not have the power to harm them. And this we believe to be attained if a fourth part at least of this mixture be water."

Abelard then gives some specific instructions on the eating of flesh by the nuns, "that their abstinence may be greater than that of monks to whom certain things are forbidden."

Flesh was not to be eaten more than once in a day, nor could several dishes of it be served at the same meal, nor any sauces added separately. It was never to be eaten more than three times a week, say, on the first, third, and fifth day, no matter what feasts intervened. "'Let us celebrate the festal day not by indulging the belly but exulting the spirit,'" Abelard adds, quoting Gregory.

The nuns were to be allowed two dishes of any vegetables and fish, since those were easily obtainable and involved little expense. But no costly spices were to be added, since the nuns must be satisfied with such things that grew in the country wherein they dwelt. Fruit was to be eaten only at supper. As medicine, however, when needed, fruits and herbs were to be brought to the table.

The pure flour of wheat was forbidden, a third part of coarser grain to be mixed with the fine. Nor were the nuns to enjoy hot loaves from the oven but were to eat those baked the day before.

Fat was forbidden on Friday, so that the nuns, contenting themselves on this day with lenten foods, might show, by their abstinence, compassion for their Bridegroom who upon that day suffered death.

If by chance, a pilgrim nun was being hospitably received, she might be offered some special dish, out of charity, and if she wished to pass it around, she might do so. But she was to sit at the high table and be served by the abbess.

"And," Abelard adds as an afterthought, "a certain disgusting habit in some monasteries is to be forbidden, namely that of wiping the hands and knives upon some part of the bread . . .

that they may spare the tablecloths and pollute the bread of the poor."

"While we do not wish to impose on the infirmity of women," Abelard says, "let the general rule regarding the abstinence of fasts suffice. But from the autumnal equinox until Easter, one meal a day shall be considered sufficient, because of the shortness of the season."

And he reminds Heloise of the scriptural saying that it is not "those things which goeth into the mouth that defileth a man, but that which cometh out of his mouth, this defileth a man."

On the subject of clothing, Abelard writes that costly garments are to be carefully avoided. Whoever seeks adornment of the body "prepares herself not for religion but for fornication . . . and thereby loses the testimony of chastity."

No clothes fit the mournful garb of penitence better than black ones, he says, nor does any wool become the bride of Christ so well as that of the lamb. And their veils are to be made not of silk but of some dyed flaxen cloth. Of these veils, Abelard adds, there shall be two: one kind for the virgins who are already consecrated, and the other for those who are not. The first shall wear the emblem of the cross imprinted on the veil, and it shall be worn on the top of their heads, and marked with white threads—after it has been consecrated by the bishop. But no other veils are to be marked with this sign.

Sufficient for covering the body is a shift, worn next to the flesh (and in which the nuns must always sleep); a woolen gown; and, when it is very cold, a mantle, which may also be used for a covering when lying down.

Because of the infestation of vermin and the accumulation of dirt that must be washed off, Abelard remarks, all these garments should be given in pairs. The length of these garments should not extend beyond the heels, so that they do not stir up dust. The sleeves should not exceed the length of the arms and hands.

The legs and feet of the nuns are to be fitted with shoes and stockings. Never, on any account, are they to go barefoot.

On their heads the nuns are to wear a white band, and over

it a black veil, and beneath, "for the tonsure of their hair," a lamb's wool bonnet, "if necessary."

As for their beds, Abelard decides that they should be allowed a mattress, a pillow, a sheet, a blanket (one), and a counter-pane. (How glad those poor nuns must have been for permission to use their mantles in the bitter cold of December, January and February!)

Abelard next takes up the importance of study. He confesses to being shocked that in the monasteries there is so little study of the Scriptures and so much instruction in singing, and at that not in the understanding of the words but in the forming of them. "As though," he says, "the bleating of sheep were more useful than the feeding of them."

The food of the soul, Abelard says, is the understanding of the Holy Scriptures. St. Benedict prescribed nothing, he says, touching the teaching or study of singing, but laid down much concerning reading, diligently appointing time for this, as he did for working. And when he provided tablets and pens for the monks, he ordered that at the beginning of Lent each monk should receive a manuscript from the library to be read through.

With many learned references, Abelard advises Heloise to give herself over to study and to imparting the knowledge she has gained, to others. "And do ye, therefore, being washed with milk, that is shining with the whiteness of chastity, abide by those rivers like doves," Abelard writes, referring to the "streams of the Word of God . . . rivers of living water."

And he goes on. "Drawing thence draughts of wisdom, ye may be able not only to say but to teach also, and to show others whither to turn their eyes, and may have power not only to behold the Bridegroom, Himself, but to describe him to others."

"If a man loves me," Abelard recites, "he will keep my word." But what words or precepts of his Lord can he keep, Abelard asks, unless he has first understood them?

He mentions that holy woman who, laying aside all else and

sitting at the Lord's feet, heard His words with those ears of understanding He requires.

And to Heloise, Abelard says: "If you are not able to be kindled to such a fervor of devotion, do you at least imitate, both in the love and the study of the Holy Writ, those blessed disciples of St. Jerome, Paula and Eustochium, at whose request the church has been enriched by so many volumes."

Thus Abelard finishes this letter to Heloise—without *Vale*, without any of the words with which even a friend signs himself at the end. He has answered her questions about a rule for her convent of nuns—answered them fully, at great length—and then, abruptly he turns away, occupied once again with God's business and his own.

22

There is no doubt that Heloise scrupulously followed the advice and instructions Abelard had sent to her, or that she was grateful to him for the help he had so painstakingly given.

Guided by these rules, as well as those of St. Benedict and St. Augustine, she conducted the Paraclete so wisely and profitably that others asked if they might form a congregation of convents under her leadership. These were the convents of Pommeraie, Treinel, and Laval, and also the congregation of St. Sulpice de la Forêt, which was made up of numerous priories in Brittany, Anjou and Touraine.

One reason that these others were so anxious to join the Paraclete was the difficulty that convents in the twelfth century had of surviving in the face of the demands made upon them by the secular powers. As soon as the convents acquired land and wealth, they aroused the interest, not to say cupidity, of other landowners. In order to protect their property, whether they wished to do so or not, the abbesses were forced to play a role in the state feudal system. This was distasteful to many of them, since it left little time to lead the peaceful life of prayer and contemplation for which they were more fitted. Not many of them had the intelligence or the strength of character of Heloise, with which she had trained herself to conduct worldly affairs as well as spiritual.

It fell upon the abbess of the Paraclete, therefore, to steer a course for all of them between the demands of the state and those of the cloister. That she did so successfully has been conceded by every authority.

By now Heloise must have fully realized that any romantic attachment between herself and Abelard was over, at least as far as he was concerned. Knowing him so well, she could see and understand the man he had become. Intellectual as ever, he was now more deeply religious than before, and, because the church had almost completely absorbed him, there was little or no room in his heart for any personal considerations beyond that of self-preservation. He would always be kind to her, as he would be to anyone who needed the advice or help that was in his power to give. But his kindness would be impersonal from now on.

Sane, wise, and moderate in his views, Abelard could still be her mentor, and her spiritual guide, too, when she needed such aid. With her he still shared the belief that faith is more important than works, and that the intention of the heart is more important than the deed. It was by this philosophy that she had been able to survive the tragedies that had befallen them both.

It was this philosophy, whether she had given it to Abelard or he to her, that formed the basis of a treatise Abelard wrote, the *Ethica, seu Scito te Ipsum,* which Rashdall in his *History of Medieval Universities* has described as "more valuable than anything the Middle Ages produced after the recovery of the *Nicomachean Ethics* of Aristotle."

It was with Abelard's philosophy, and the rule he drew up for her use at the Paraclete, that Heloise had to be content. For with the man Abelard, the object of her sexual obsession as well as her devotion, she could have no more traffic. If she had, during the first years she was in the order, beat her fists against the stone walls of the convent, if she had stormed against the cruelty of God for dissolving her marriage, if she had poured out her heart in those first letters to Abelard, begging, hoping for something—though she herself knew not what it could be—all that was over. Gone were the delusions that anything could be changed.

The man Abelard whom she had loved, and whom she still loved, was no more hers than were any of the saints to whom she prayed, no more than the impersonal monks who were called in on occasion to assist the nuns at their rites, no more than any other pilgrim traveling along the same stony road to salvation.

But give him up entirely, she could not. By the one bond that still linked them, his interest in the Paraclete, she again called him back to her, if only by the written word. She sent him a long series of questions concerning points that had puzzled her in her study of the Scriptures, and asked that he clarify them for her so that she could best instruct her nuns.

Known as "The Problems of Heloise," these questions have come down to us as one of her few authentic writings apart from the letters to Abelard. Aside from showing us the types of theological question that occupied the minds of scholars in those days, they reveal the extent of Heloise's reading, and her critical attitude, which found it impossible to accept the Gospels until she could understand and believe them. This questioning attitude is one she may have acquired from Abelard, although, on the other hand, it may have been one of the qualities of her mind that first attracted him to her.

There were forty-two questions, in each of which Heloise stated the problem concisely. She was, for example, troubled by the conflicting Gospel versions of the denial of Jesus by Peter. Her sense of justice was disturbed by the parable of Jesus cursing the fig tree for not bearing fruit out of season. And in the story of the woman who was taken in adultery, with reference to the saying of Jesus, "Let him without sin among you cast the first stone," Heloise wanted to know if that did not imply that all punishment is to be condemned, since there is no mortal without sin.

Whether the "Problems of Heloise" were written in order to prove to Abelard that she had followed his advice and was now devoting herself wholeheartedly to study and contemplation, or because she genuinely wanted specific points clarified for her and the nuns of the Paraclete, Abelard answered each one of them carefully and brilliantly—all forty-two of them. Some of his answers were as brief as the questions, some of them as long as treatises, but in all he displayed once again his power to twist words to his meaning. Whether Heloise was satisfied with the answers, whether they cleared the issues for her, we do not know. But at least, by these means, she heard from Abelard again.

It would appear, from the effort Abelard put into these answers to Heloise's questions, that he was infinitely relieved to find her mind turned to matters of religion and away from the personal relationship that he found so painful now. As long as she continued to appeal to him as her spiritual adviser and nothing else—above all not as her lover and husband—he was able to respond with something like tenderness and affection.

It was Heloise, it is said, who was responsible for Abelard's writing his *Hexameron*, which dealt with, and attempted to explain in detail, the six days of the world's creation, as described in the book of *Genesis*.

After the *Hexameron*, Abelard answered Heloise's request for some special hymns to be sung at the Paraclete, since, she declared, the translation of the psalms which they were using was obsolete; many lacked titles and authorship, and some of the hymns scanned so badly that it was impossible to fit the words to the music. Unfortunately, the letter of Heloise making this request has been lost, but the tenor of it is implicit in Abelard's reply.

He applied himself so diligently to this request that the nuns of the Paraclete received, over a period of time and in three separate bundles, a total of 133 hymns, composed by Abelard for their use.

(These hymns, known as *Petri Abaelardi peripatetici hymnarius paraclitensis, sive hymnorum libelli tres* were edited by Dreves in 1891, from the text of the fifteenth- or sixteenth-century manuscript known as the *Breviary of Abelard, or of the Paraclete*, which was discovered in the middle of the nineteenth century at the library of Chaumont. They became well known and were in use at least until the thirteenth century.)

Although it was apparent to Heloise how great an effort these hymns had cost Abelard, and how much of his time they consumed, she made yet another request, this time asking him for some sermons to be used at the convent. He explained in a note

how difficult it was for him to find the leisure to comply with her
request, and that he would have to write them in haste, with little
attention to style. And yet he did send her a collection of sermons, some of which have been collected by D'Amboise, including one called *In natali innocentum*, bringing the number of
sermons to thirty-four.

In all of the notes that accompanied the hymns and sermons,
Abelard asked the nuns to pray for him as a return for the
burdens they placed upon him by their requests. And with the
last of the sermons, he added an ending which moved Heloise
deeply:

"Farewell in the Lord, thou his handmaid, once dear to me in
the world, and now most dear to me in Christ; once my wife in
the flesh, now my sister in the spirit, and my companion in the
religious life."

If she had used her wits to find means to attract Abelard's
attention, and if any grain of recognition was better than the
silence that is the death of love, Heloise had achieved her aim.
At least Abelard was not allowed to forget her, at least he remembered her with tenderness, at least her name was still written
in his heart.

It is not known whether Abelard actually visited the Paraclete
during this exchange of questions and answers, but in all proba-
bility he did not. He was still living officially at the monastery
of St. Gildas, though he was freer to travel than he had been.
On the other hand, he was suffering still more acutely from those
fears for his safety which he had expressed in his *Historia
Calamitatum*. When he traveled abroad at this time he was convinced it was at the risk of being murdered by his own monks
or by strangers they had hired to do away with him.

His interest in the oratory of the Paraclete persisted, however,
and he was always ready to do whatever lay in his power to help
the nuns whom he had placed there. However Heloise prayed
for more than this, it is not likely her prayers were granted, or
that she was permitted to have any more of Abelard than his
handwriting on the epistles he sent her.

Whatever her private sorrow, the abbess of the Paraclete was too busy now to have time for self-indulgence. The population of her convent had grown rapidly. The number of nuns varied according to the prominence, prestige and accessibility of the different convents. Some accepted only women of noble birth, others were less exclusive. In the twelfth century a convent of sixty nuns was considered large. Less than half that number was the average. In the beginning, the Paraclete had less than a dozen nuns, but as its property increased and the fame of Heloise spread, its population grew to sixty.

Many of these women had entered the convent as children, bound over by their parents to the religious life. Medieval convents did not have a novitiate such as there is today. There was no probationary period, since, if they had come as children they were already bound over, and if they came later, mostly as widows, they were permitted to pronounce their vows after a period of four weeks. Profession was received, usually by the abbess herself, in a simple rite.

In addition to the duties laid down for the abbess in the *Regla* of St. Benedict, and those suggested by Abelard, Heloise supervised the education of the children. After religious instruction, the subjects taught were Latin, reading, music, and the womanly arts of embroidery, weaving, etc. Heloise was especially well-equipped to teach Latin, reading, and music, and relegated the rest to her subordinates.

In the earliest Benedictine convents, the nuns performed all the necessary work about the place themselves. But as the hours for prayers increased, and the devotion to choir service grew, to say nothing of the increased attention to scholarship encouraged by Heloise, there was less time or inclination for menial work. Since servants were not permitted, the nuns accepted lay sisters to work in the kitchen, the bakery, and the laundry. These made vows of obedience to the abbess and bound themselves to work. In addition to these lay sisters, it was necessary to acquire lay brothers to do the work of the fields, and these dwelt outside the convent walls, some in farm buildings especially constructed for them.

The Paraclete lived on the produce of its estates, which soon included widely dispersed farms and vineyards that were leased to tenants and provided a not inconsiderable income. Heloise thus had to occupy herself with buying, exchanging and mortgaging properties, even if, as is likely, she had a provost monk to advise her.

Although we have no actual description of Heloise in her role of abbess of the Paraclete, there is a description, given by one Wilbert of Gembloux, of another convent and another abbess of the period, or perhaps a little later, which can be applied to Heloise.

"The convent is rich in religious zeal and also in income. . . . The mother is kind to all, gives good advice to everyone who asks it, resolves the most difficult problems presented to her, writes books, instructs her sisters, leads sinners back to the right paths and is always fully occupied."

We have said that with such a busy life there could be no time for private sorrow. And yet, for the private sorrow there is, perhaps, always time. Occupied as she was during the long day and most of the night, there were still moments of great weariness when the guards were let down and the image of Abelard came before her. When, for an interval, the voices of the nuns chanting were not to be heard, and the tinkling of bells in the dark corridors was in abeyance, she would recall, fleetingly, the period when she was in the world with Abelard; when, like any other married pair, they sat together in an ordinary house in Brittany and watched over their child.

The vows that Heloise had made when she took the veil she kept faithfully. But did not that vow she had made earlier, in the church in Paris, before her uncle and a few selected friends, the marriage vow, bind her forever to Abelard, body and soul? Could mere intention sever those bonds?

We know that they were never successfully severed, from the words of Peter the Venerable when later he attempted to console her. But we hear no more from Heloise of the fierce struggle that still went on in her breast, the warfare of the heart.

23

In the year 1136, Abelard was enjoying a return to favor. It was with the consent of the pope that he was able to leave the monastery of St. Gildas to appear once more before large classes of students in Paris. No lesser authority could have released him from his duties as abbot.

After the miseries of the years he had spent in that remote part of Brittany, the joy of functioning again in the role for which he was most fitted, was great. It added to his joy and relief that Heloise convinced him she was ready to turn her back upon the irreconcilable past and devote herself to religion.

For three or four years Abelard was free to teach, and to devote his time to writing books and correcting those of his already in circulation, such as his *Introductio ad Theologiam*, *Sic et Non*, and *Scito te Ipsum*. These were being more widely read than they had been before, in spite of Abelard's long absence from the intellectual scene.

Returning in the garb of monk to Mount Ste. Genevieve, Abelard had lost none of his brilliance, magnetism, or persuasiveness. Students flocked to him, as before, by the hundreds, perhaps thousands, because he had something to give them that the other teachers lacked. This was clarity, but it was also his fresh approach to truth, expressed so beautifully in that famous voice, but expressed unemotionally and in terms of the purest logic that scholars could appreciate.

In *The Medieval Mind*, Henry Osborn Taylor says that Abelard's nature was set upon understanding all things through reason, even the mysteries of faith: "He does not say, or quite think, that he will disbelieve what he cannot understand; but his reasoning and temper point to the conclusion."

The titles given by Abelard to his various treatises, Taylor points out, are "indicative of the critical insistency of his nature." He gave his *Ethica* the subtitle of *Scito te Ipsum:* "Know thyself —understand thy good and ill intentions, and what may be vice or virtue in thee."

Throughout this book, the discussion of right and wrong directs itself to the consideration of human nature showing that Abelard was capable of a lofty insight touching the relationship between God and man. In this book he writes: "Penitence is truly fruitful when grief and contrition proceed from love of God, regarded as benignant, rather than from fear of penalties. Sin cannot endure with this contrition of heart: for sin is contempt of God, or consent to evil, and the love of God . . . suffers no ill."

Some of Abelard's writings have been regarded as the work of a dialectician rather than of a moralist. It is evident from these books that Abelard disapproved of the blind acceptance of faith handed down to children by their parents, and, as Taylor says, "the narrowness of mind which keeps men from perceiving the possible truth in others' opinions."

The work on theology which had been burnt at the council of Soissons, in 1121, Abelard now rewrote and presented in another form, with the title *Theologia Christiana.*

The first book of this *Theologia* gives the authority for Abelard's views on the Trinity. The second book defends his use of the testimonies of profane writers on the subject: "Nothing is more needful for the defense of our faith than that, as against the importunities of all the infidels, we should have witness from themselves wherewith to refute them."

At the beginning of Book III, Abelard makes the statement: "We set the faith of the blessed Trinity as the foundation of all good." And he proceeds from there to a defense of dialectics and a denunciation of those who misuse it.

From this juncture, it has been pointed out by Henry Osborn Taylor and others, Abelard's work becomes more dialectical. While he continues to quote authorities, he does not hesitate to discuss the deepest mysteries, including the Trinity—in a way that alarmed men like Bernard, who wished acceptance of the faith, with rhetoric but without discussion.

The more one comes to know Abelard, through his works, through the famous story of his calamities, through his relationship with Heloise, the more one is impressed with his fearlessness in respect to intellectual matters. But one also becomes more and more impressed with his unfortunate ability to annoy his so-called peers, and to bring upon himself all those catastrophes of which he was human enough to complain bitterly.

Had he not given his word that if allowed to lecture, he would avoid theological subjects? Otherwise, would he have been granted permission by the pope to conduct classes, as he was doing? After all, his fame as a teacher of logic, of dialectics, and of other nonclerical subjects, was enough to fill his classes. And yet, just as he had previously touched on the sensitive point of the Trinity when it was most dangerous for him to do so, now he was led by some inner compulsion to touch on equally sensitive spots of current theology.

It has been said that the heresy of one age may be the accepted doctrine of the next. But Abelard would have been a thorn in the flesh to authorities even if he had been reborn say, in the thirteenth or fourteenth century, and even if his method and opinions of the twelfth century had then become acceptable. His need to speak the truth as he saw it was more imperative for him than for most men. And he was certainly possessed of an inordinate compulsion to disturb his rivals, if not to completely overturn them.

And so, just when he might have enjoyed a little peace, and basked for a time at least in the glory of his fame as a scholar, Abelard evoked the wrath of one who had shown that he could be an implacable enemy as well as brother—none other than Bernard of Clairvaux, now one of the most powerful men in France.

As long as Abelard dwelt in obscurity, Bernard could afford to ignore him. There were more important things to occupy churchmen than the chastisement of one muted voice crying out in the wilderness of St. Gildas, in far-off Brittany. As long as Abelard continued to occupy himself with the poor struggling nuns at the Paraclete, he was left alone, and everybody, including Bernard, felt relieved.

But now here he was again, not only lifting his head but preaching his unorthodox views in Paris before a multitude of such young men as Bernard required for himself. And worse even than that, he was writing and rewriting books, which could not be said to omit those questions of theology on which he had promised to be silent.

Such audacity was not to be tolerated, Bernard decided. It must be stopped at once, and by any means. Many of Bernard's friends were quick to agree with him.

The attack against Abelard began in March 1140, with a formal letter from William of St. Thierry, one of Bernard's closest friends, bringing charges against Abelard before Bernard and the bishop of Chartres. These charges were as follows:

"Pierre Abelard seized the moment when all the masters of ecclesiastical doctrine have disappeared from the scene of the world to conquer a place for himself in the schools, and to create there an exclusive domination. He treats Holy Scripture as though it were dialectics. It is a matter with him of personal invention and annual novelty. He is the censor and not the disciple of the faith; the corrector and not the imitator of the authorized masters."

In other words, Abelard's innovations were becoming dangerous not only in the schools, but also to the papal court in Rome. There was no one who would act to stop him, Bernard's friends pointed out, or who *could* act, save Bernard. In words which Henry Adams attributes to them, they said, "This man fears you. He dreads you! If you shut your eyes whom will he fear? . . . The evil has become too public to allow a correction limited to amicable discipline and secret warnings."

To further convince Bernard—if that were necessary—William

marked thirteen passages in one of Abelard's books, which may have been the *Introductio ad Theologiam*, all of which passages he considered heretical. He also implied that there might be even offensive words in Abelard's *Sic et Non*, which apparently neither he nor Bernard had read.

Bernard was busy just then, since it was the Easter season. But after the holy days were over, he went to see Abelard, not once but twice, to try to persuade him amicably that he should modify his views. One wonders where these meetings were held and what occurred between these two, both leaders of men from diametrically opposite camps. What mention there is of these meetings indicates that they were cordial enough, but they did not produce any change in the beliefs of either man.

Abelard still insisted that he taught theology because his students demanded it, for "they did not want mere words, but would believe only what they could understand." And Bernard accused Abelard of seeing nothing as an enigma, but "looking at everything face to face."

Abelard claimed, for one thing, that "all God does He wills necessarily and does necessarily; for His goodness is such that it pushes Him necessarily to do all the good He can, and the best He can, and the quickest He can . . . therefore it is of necessity that God willed and made the world."

Some say that this pure logic of Abelard's was bound to be necessitarian or it ceased to be logical. It could allow of no chance. Bernard regarded it as the equivalent of saying that Abelard's world, being the best and the only one possible, need trouble itself no more about God, church, or man. Bernard believed strongly that the scholastic method was false and mischievous, and that the longer it was followed the greater the mischief. He believed that, because dialectics led to false conclusions, faith led to the right ones.

Feeling as strongly as he did about this "mischief" of Abelard's, he could easily have ordered, through the pope, Abelard's submission, his return to St. Gildas in Brittany—and his silence. But Bernard was reluctant to cause any more scandal in the

church, and so he went through the forms of friendly negoti-
ation with Abelard, hoping to change him.

It was only when Abelard refused to meet Bernard's proposal,
which, in effect, would have meant his utter extinction as a
teacher and a thinker, that Bernard started his attack. He began
to write letters to the pope and the cardinals in Rome, letters in
which he let loose the full force of his fury against Abelard,
letters that were both eloquent and vile in their accusations.

Abelard may have wished to ignore these slanderous accusations, which came, of course, to his knowledge, but his scholars
were indignant and would not let him. And for his scholars Abelard wrote the following in his own defense:

"A new calumny have my rivals lately devised, because I write
upon the dialectic art; affirming that it is not lawful for a
Christian to treat of things which do not pertain to the faith.
Not only they say that this science does not prepare us for the
faith, but that it destroys faith by the implication of its arguments.

"But it is strange if I must not discuss what is permitted them
to read. If they allow that the art of dialectics militates against
faith, surely they deem it not to be science. For the science of
truth is the comprehension of things, whose *species* is the
wisdom in which faith consists. Truth is not opposed to truth.
For not as falsehood may be opposed to falsehood, or evil to
evil, can the true be opposed to the true, or the good to the
good; but rather all good things are in accord.

"All knowledge is good, even that which relates to evil, because a righteous man must have knowledge. Since he must
guard against evil, it is necessary that he should know it before-
hand, otherwise he could not shun it. Though an act be evil,
knowledge regarding it is good; though it be evil to sin, it is
good to know the sin which otherwise we could not shun. Nor
is the science *mathematica* to be deemed evil, whose practice,
astrology, is evil. . . .

"It is therefore not wrong to know, but to do; the evil is to
be referred to the act and not to the knowledge. Hence we are
convinced that all knowledge, which indeed comes from God

alone and from His bounty, is good. Wherefore the study of every science should be conceded to be good, because that which is good comes from it; and especially must one insist upon the study of that *doctrina* by which the greater truth is known. This is dialectic, whose function is to distinguish between every truth and falsity: as leader in all knowledge, it holds the primacy and rule of all philosophy. The same also is shown to be needed to the Catholic faith, which cannot without its aid resist the sophistries of the schismatics."

What aroused Bernard and his cohorts was not so much Abelard's opinions as his critical spirit. Bernard held that "faith does not discuss, but believes," and to him any departure from this was rank heresy. The very thought of Abelard standing before thousands of young men, and asking them to question those truths which Bernard believed to be unquestionable, was quite enough to try the patience of a saint, especially so many-sided a saint as Bernard of Clairvaux.

When Abelard's students learned that on the Sunday after Whitsuntide, King Louis VII was coming to Sens to inspect the relics in the cathedral there, and that there would surely be a large and important assembly for the occasion, they asked the archbishop of Sens to consent to a public dispute between Bernard and their teacher, at which Abelard would have an opportunity to defend his faith publicly.

Surprisingly enough, the archbishop agreed and wrote to Bernard, inviting him to take part in a public debate. This, Bernard had no intention of doing. In the first place, he had passed along to the pope all responsibility for Abelard's behavior. Was it not the pope's concern to bring heretics to trial and to punish them? He, Bernard, had given Abelard the benefit of his advice, and that opinionated, arrogant rebel had refused to take it. Now it was up to Rome to deal with him. Besides, Bernard knew perfectly well that in a public debate he would be no match for a master of dialectics who, by the process of cold logic, could make white appear to be black, to please himself!

He therefore refused the archbishop's invitation, saying, by way of excuse, that he disapproved of arguing on questions of faith. He suggested that this was a case to be judged by bishops, and not by a monk and an abbot. However, he immediately went to the trouble of writing a circular letter to all the bishops in the province of Sens, persuading them to attend the assembly and to beware of the falseness and cleverness of Abelard.

The council opened on Monday, June 3, 1140, the day after the royal inspection of the cathedral's treasures. Rarely had the cathedral of Sens been so filled. Crowds of people, unable to find room inside, gathered on the steps of the entrance and even on the streets. Within, there were the king, his royal party, and important personages of both church and state, along with ecclesiastics of every rank, from archbishops to the lowest clerk, who were able to gain entrance.

Abelard, who had good reason to hold any council in dread since that other council at Soissons which had such dire consequences for him, entered the cathedral bravely enough, followed by a band of his loyal students. A glance from his penetrating brown eyes revealed to him the extent to which the great Bernard had packed the house, literally and figuratively, with those who, because of the nature of their calling, would be on the side of authority and hostile to Abelard. Many of them, not excluding the king, were indebted to Bernard for part of their power and prestige.

And, to crown the situation, there was Bernard, who had changed his mind about facing Abelard, and now sat in the very center of the council like a prosecuting attorney. He opened the assembly himself by producing seventeen statements taken from Abelard's books, some of them out of context, and demanding that they be read aloud and that Abelard be asked to deny or correct them.

It was with a sickening sense of despair that Abelard recognized at once that he would have even less chance of a judicial hearing now than he had had at Soissons twenty years before. The reading had only just begun when Abelard cried out for it to be stopped.

To the amazement of all, he announced that he would have nothing to do with this council, nor with any judge whatever except one—the pope—and that he would appeal to him in Rome. So saying, he turned and with great dignity, left the cathedral.

Abelard has given no account of this incident, but others have, and it would appear that no sooner had he left the cathedral than Bernard seized the opportunity to ask that the council pass judgement on Abelard's works, leaving the man himself to be judged by the pope.

It was after dinner that the volume of Abelard's *Theology* was read in a droning voice by one of the clerks. The bishops, who had dined well and, not being abstemious like Bernard, had also drunk much wine, nodded over the reading or, talking among themselves, made jokes. And finally they grew impatient.

They began to growl, "*Damnamus—namus*" and so made an end to the whole business. The works of Abelard were thus condemned, and everyone was free to go home and sleep, conscious of Bernard's approval—and his favor.

It was naive of Abelard to expect that an appeal to Rome would help him. Innocent II had once been friendly toward him, but times had changed since then. Bernard's influence and power had grown, and Abelard's had dwindled. Bernard was on the side of conservatism and order, and Abelard was first, last, and always a rebel—who gave no peace to anyone, least of all himself.

He was, according to most of those who have written about Abelard, no heretic in the broad sense. He believed in the church, the Trinity, the Gospels, and the true Christian way of life. But in a narrower sense, by the ordinary definition of the word heresy—"an opinion or doctrine at variance with fundamental truths commonly received as orthodox"—there was room for a reasonable doubt. There was also a factor which Abelard seems not to have considered. As Henry Adams has put it, Innocent II owed everything to Bernard, while Abelard owed everything to Innocent.

Bernard, much wiser in the way of politics, lost no time helping the pope to make a decision regarding Abelard. As soon as the council of Sens had ended, Bernard dispatched two letters to Rome. One was, ostensibly, from the archbishop of Sens, and the other from the archbishop of Rheims, but there seems to be little doubt that both were from the hand of the great Bernard. These letters contained a one-sided account of what had occurred at the council on June 3rd.

Another letter, signed by Bernard, implored the pope to wreak vengeance upon an enemy of the church. Abelard was a viper, he wrote, who had crawled out of his hole, and, having one head cut off at Soissons, had grown seven more. He was, according to Bernard, "a monk without rule; a prelate without responsibility; an abbot without discipline . . . disputing with boys, conversing with women." Then, with an effort to control his anger, which was verging on the petty, Bernard continued his attack by grandly accusing Abelard of insisting upon understanding and explaining, before believing.

"The faith of the righteous believes," Bernard said, "it does not dispute. But that man, suspicious of God (*Deum habens suspectum*) has no mind to believe what his own reason has not previously argued."

Not content with all this, Bernard made sure that the pope's advisers should know how to think, and so he wrote a letter to every cardinal of influence, warning them to show no mercy to the miserable offender who sought justice from them.

The savagery of Bernard's attack aroused the calm and tolerant abbot of Cluny, Peter the Venerable, to turn on the great prelate, who had always been considered charitable, with the rebuke; "You perform all the difficult religious duties. You fast; you watch; you suffer. But you will not endure the easy ones. You do not love!"

Abelard had other defenders, perhaps the strangest of whom was Arnold of Brescia, a monk of the utmost austerity, who, upon being exiled from Rome for troublemaking, joined Abelard in Paris. After the trial he favored Abelard's cause with Cardinal Jacintus, and spoke out against Bernard of Clairvaux. After Abelard had left Paris, it was Arnold who taught the Holy

Scriptures to Abelard's classes at Mount Ste. Genevieve. But the classes soon dwindled to a handful of poor students, who begged alms publicly from door to door. The name of Bernard was enough to frighten scholars now, and young men had to be careful.

The charges that Bernard made against Abelard may have been in themselves literally true, but they were not actually very serious, since neither faith nor morals were involved. As Henry Adams has said: "On the other hand, Abelard never affected or aspired to be a saint, while Bernard always affected to judge the acts and motives of his fellow creatures from a standpoint of more than worldly charity. Bernard had no right to Abelard's vices since he claimed to be judged by a higher standard; but his temper was none of the best, and his pride was something of the worst."

Whatever the motives, it was this so-called trial held at Sens in June of the year 1140, controlled as it was by Bernard, which marked the end for Abelard.

24

Abelard was sixty-one that summer when he set out for Rome to plead his own case before Pope Innocent II. He was worn out both emotionally and physically with the strain of the affair at Sens, and he was forced to make frequent stops at monasteries along the way. A skin affliction caused him great annoyance and disturbed his sleep at night, so at each stop he was forced to linger until he gathered enough strength to continue the long journey.

The pope, warned in advance of this impending visit, and dreading the need to face his former friend, managed to forestall it. Only six weeks after the council of Sens, Innocent sent an edict addressed to the archbishops of Sens and Rheims, and to the abbot of Clairvaux, condemning the selections from Abelard's works that he had been asked to judge. More than this, he imposed on Abelard, whom he called a heretic, an order for perpetual silence. He was to be sequestered in a monastery, and all copies of his books were to be burned. And, lest any voice be raised in protest, he decreed that all of Abelard's followers and defenders were to be excommunicated.

Abelard was traveling through Burgundy at the time, unaware of this harsh sentence. Needing refreshment of the spirit as well as of the body, he arrived at the monastery of Cluny, and was welcomed with open arms by that most gracious and understanding of men, Peter the Venerable.

Learned himself, Peter admired and respected Abelard. Of a

liberal turn of mind, he could understand the essential religious orthodoxy of this philosopher and teacher who had been accused of heresy. Peter was a great prelate; he could understand and pity human suffering, and his sympathies went out at once to the man who had been so ruthlessly hunted down. He received him now not only with affection and compassion, but with a sincere reverence and respect which must have meant much to a tired and disillusioned Abelard who had come to the end of his strength.

And yet, being wise in the ways of the world, Peter the Venerable persuaded Abelard to make his peace with Bernard, and to retract whatever he had said or written that the church found offensive. Abelard agreed to this up to a point. He wrote his *Apologia*, a confession of faith, in which he declared himself, as a true son of the faith, willing to retract any errors he had made. However, he accused his enemies of malicious slander and a perversion of his real views, which contained nothing that could or should have been termed heresy.

It was at about this time that Raynard, the abbot of Citeaux, visited Cluny, and it is thought that he was the one who broke the news of the pope's edict to Abelard and Peter. If so, it was after his recovery from the shock that Abelard let himself be persuaded by Peter and Raynard to attempt a reconciliation with Bernard and to write his *Apologia*.

At any rate, Abelard was tired. The effort to continue a fight, in which the decision had already twice gone against him, seemed hardly worth while. Here at the abbey of Cluny there was peace and understanding and rest. He asked permission to join the congregation and it was granted to him.

As a monk of Cluny, holding his tongue and conforming in every way to the rules that were established, the world and his enemies might forget him. That was his one desire. Let others carry on the fight for reason, let the young men, eager for truth, find other teachers, other methods. Once he had written surpassingly lovely poems, sung them, and given them to others to sing. When he was done, he had put by the lute. On the philosophy of religion he had had his say. Let others speak now;

Abelard was silent. His lips moved only to recite the litany, only to offer up the prayers of the day or the night hours—to God.

Just a fragment of the *Apologia*, his Confession of Faith, has come down to us, although it has been called the most moving and restrained piece of writing Abelard ever did. It ends: "I have founded my knowledge on that rock whereon Christ built his Church. . . .

"This then is the faith by which I abide, and from which I draw the firmness of my hope. Strongly anchored thereto, I fear not the barking of Scylla, I laugh at the whirlpools of Charybdis, I dread not the death-bringing harmonies of the sirens. If the hurricane breaks, I shall not be shaken. If the winds rage, I shall not be moved. For I am founded upon the immovable rock."

It is perhaps surprising to find that this *Apologia*, written at the urgency of Peter the Venerable, in the safety of Cluny, was addressed to Heloise. "Heloise, my sister," it began, followed by a brief explanation that it was written "so that anxious care and all evasions" might be banished from the heart in her breast.

Why did he not seek the safety of that breast and those tender arms when he grew tired on his way to Rome? Could it have been that, aware of the pack that was on his trail, he had no wish to lead them to the door of the Paraclete?

How much it would have meant to Heloise to know that her beloved was safe at last from a world whose pettiness he could never understand! Her anxieties for him could at least in some measure be lightened by the knowledge that Peter the Venerable, who had shown and was still to show how good a friend he was to them both, was looking after Abelard's needs as well as she could have done—no, better, because Peter was strong and could deal with the world, and she was a woman and vulnerable.

During the two years of life that were left to Abelard, it is not known whether any messages passed between Heloise and himself, and, although the distance between Cluny and the Paraclete was inconsiderable, it is almost certain that they never met again.

For the manner in which Abelard conducted himself, and the

way in which death came to him, we have the words of Peter the Venerable, in a letter addressed to Heloise.

"A brief word cannot tell of his holy, humble and devout way of life among us, as Cluny bears strong witness. For, unless I am mistaken, I do not recollect that I have seen his like, in the appearance and actions of humility, so much that, to the very discerning, neither St. Germain would appear more abject, nor St. Martin, himself, poorer. And when, at my command, he took a superior rank in that great assembly of our brothers, he seemed the least in plainness of his apparel.

"I wondered often, as he went before me in processions with the others, according to custom, nay, I was almost astounded that a man of so great and famous a name could thus belittle himself, could thus humble himself. And while there are certain of those who profess religion, who desire that the religious garments which they wear should be exceedingly sumptuous, he was sparing of these, and, content with a simple garment of any kind, he asked for nothing more.

"He observed this practice also in food, and in drink, and in all care of his own body, and he condemned in his words and in his actions I do not say the superfluous only, but everything except what was really necessary, both for himself and for everyone.

"His reading was continuous, his prayer frequent, his silence perpetual, except when familiar intercourse with the brothers or public discussion in their assembly pressed upon him to speak to them about divine things. . . .

"And what more can I say? His mind, his tongue, his labor, always serving God, always philosophical, ever more learned, he meditated, taught and spoke. Living thus with us for some time, this simple and upright man, fearing God, and withdrawing from evil, consecrated the last days of his life to God."

Abelard did not actually die at the abbey of Cluny. When his infirmities became worse (Peter the Venerable mentions that he was "troubled with scabies and certain discomforts of the body.") he was sent to St. Marcel les Châlons, which, of all the regions in Burgundy, was then thought to have the most healthful climate. There, as far as his strength allowed, Abelard re-sumed his studies, forever bent over his books, reading, writing, or dictating, when he was not praying.

The end, when it came, was swift and merciful, and occurred while he was among his books and not in bed. As Peter the Venerable described it: "In these holy exercises the coming of that angelic visitor found him, and discovered him not sleeping, like many, but vigilant. It found him truly watchful and summoned him, not as the foolish, but as the wise virgin, to the marriage feast of eternity. For he brought with him a lamp full of oil, that is, a conscience filled with the testimony of a holy life."

He was fully conscious when he received the last rites of the church, in the presence of the brothers of the little monastery of St. Marcel.

To further comfort Heloise when this news should reach her, the kindly abbot of Cluny wrote: "Thus dear and venerable sister in God, he to whom you are united, after your tie in the flesh, by the better and stronger bond of the divine love; he with whom and under whom you have served the Lord, the Lord now takes in your place, like another you, and warms in His bosom; and, for the day of His coming, when shall sound the voice of the archangel, and the triumpet of God descending from heaven, He keeps him to restore him to you by His grace."

Thus, on April 21, 1142, Abelard, born Pierre du Pallet, de-parted this life and entered into a peace that he had never known on earth.

"For a little while," wrote Remusat, "the veil had been lifted, then it closed over the mystery of this man whom the love of God and the hate of men had broken, yet left greater in his ruin."

And of this man, even William of St. Thierry, he who had begun the last attack against him, said: "and yet I loved him."

25

The news of Abelard's death was brought to Heloise by a monk of Cluny, named Thibaud, whom Peter the Venerable had dispatched with the tidings.

She may have been with a class of children, teaching them to read the notes and words of a hymn Abelard had composed for the convent, when the porteress came to announce that a monk from Cluny had arrived with a message. She may have been in her own study, reading or meditating. But when she rose and followed the porteress to the gate, she had a premonition of what that message contained. And as she walked swiftly along the stone corridor, in her black robes and veil, her hands clasped at her breast, her lips moved in prayer that she be given the strength to receive the tidings with courage—or even a prayer that what she feared the most might not have happened.

When she reached the porteress' lodge and saw the hand of Thibaud stretched toward her in a gesture of sympathy, she bowed her head. There was no need for words. Abelard was dead, and the world, for Heloise, stood still for a moment, until the fortitude she had prayed for returned.

She felt very much alone now. For years she had lived with the hope, sometimes very dim, that she might see Abelard again. There was always a way of getting news of him, at least. And there had been those few precious times when she had been granted the supreme joy of his presence. But now that hope was dead, as Abelard was dead.

It was some consolation that he had thought of her toward the end of his life, and that he had addressed his *Apologia* to her, even though it was intended to be read by Bernard and the other church dignitaries. This was proof that he had wanted her, above all others, to understand him—Abelard, the man as well as the philosopher.

And there was the smaller comfort, the realization that she would no longer lie awake at night while her convent slept, worrying about the man she loved—whether he was being properly cared for, whether he got his needed rest, or whether there were kind hands to provide ointments for his tormented body. Her beloved was safe at last, and beyond need of those physical comforts she would so gladly have provided for him.

There was still something that she could do for Abelard, however. He had asked, not once but several times, in those long epistles to her and her sisters, that his body should be brought to the Paraclete for burial, no matter what the circumstances of his death or where it had occurred.

No place, he had said, could be as safe for the soul of one who bitterly repented his sins as that which was consecrated to the true Comforter; and no more fitting burial could be found for him, he had said, than among women devoted to their vows, who would pray over his body for the salvation of his soul. "Thus," he had written, "they might show by their prayers for the dead man how they had loved him when alive."

Heloise now wrote to Peter, asking for help in carrying out Abelard's wish. She knew it would be a difficult one to fulfill.

But so great was the affection of Peter the Venerable for Abelard and for Heloise that he went himself to the abbey of St. Marcel, accompanied by several of his trusted monks, and managed to have the body of Abelard removed by stealth, without the knowledge of the monks there, who wished to keep to themselves the relics of so famous a man. And it was Peter also who brought the body to the Paraclete and gave it to Heloise for burial. Concerning this deed, there has come down to us the contents of a letter which Heloise wrote to Peter.

"By God's mercy, we have been visited by the favor of your

graciousness. We are glad, kindest father, and we glory that your greatness condescended to our insignificance. A visit from you is an honor even to the great. . . .

"I cannot tell in words, or even comprehend in thought, how beneficial and how sweet your coming was to me. You, our abbot and our lord, celebrated mass with us on the Calends of last December. You commended us to the Holy Spirit. You nourished us with the Divine Word. *You gave us the body of our master and confirmed that gift from Cluny.*

"To me also, unworthy to be your servant, though by word and letter you have called me sister, you gave as a pledge of sincere love the privilege of a tricenarium, to be performed by the brethren of Cluny, after my death, for the benefit of my soul. You have promised to confirm this under your seal. May you fulfill this, my lord.

"Might it please you also to send me that other sealed roll, containing the absolution of the master, that I may hang it on his tomb.

"Remember also, for the love of God, our, and your, Astrolabe, to obtain for him a prebend from the bishop of Paris, or another.

"Farewell. May God preserve you and grant to us sometime your presence."

The good Peter answered with a warm and affectionate letter, confirming his gift of the tricenarium. He also sent the record of Abelard's absolution, which read: "I, Peter, abbot of Cluny, who received Peter Abelard to be a monk in Cluny, and granted his body, secretly transported, to the Abbess Heloise and the nuns of the Paraclete, absolve him, in the performance of my office (*pro officio*) by the authority of the omnipotent God and all the saints, from all his sins."

As for the third request, that he secure a prebend for the son of Abelard and Heloise, he wrote that he would do his best, but that it would not be easy to persuade a bishop of one of the great churches to part with one of the coveted "livings," as they all seemed to have nephews or sons whom they wished so to favor. But he promised, for her sake, to do what he could in this matter, and as soon as he could arrange it.

This mention of Astrolabe comes as a relief to chroniclers who have searched, in vain, for documents dealing with him. In those wonderful letters which passed between Heloise and Abelard there is no mention of the boy who was now a man.

We know that Heloise was forced to part with her child before the fateful return to Paris. But it is difficult to believe that so warm and tender a woman did not show deep concern for his well-being during the years when he was growing up in Brittany.

The childhood of Astrolabe must have been a fairly happy one, in spite of the absence of his parents. Brought up by Abelard's sister, Denise, with her own children, he would have enjoyed the freedom of the grounds of a medieval castle, playing among the great trees and beside the rushing streams. With an affectionate family to replace the one he might have had under normal circumstances, he was undoubtedly very well off.

But how did he fare as he grew older, as he began to understand who he was and why he had been deprived of his own parents? Did messages pass between Heloise and her sister-in-law at Le Pallet? None have survived, although they may have been carried back and forth by visiting monks or travelers. There is reason to believe, especially from the form of Heloise's request to Peter the Venerable, that Astrolabe, having received the available instruction in his aunt's household, entered a monastery to continue his education, with a view to becoming a cleric, as his father had been.

This being probably the case, it is understandable that Heloise would have seized the opportunity, even in that letter of gratitude, to appeal to the abbot of Cluny for a benefice for her son. She speaks of Astrolabe as "our, and your," as if, her son having now lost his own father, Peter would share in the responsibility of providing for his future, and would use his powerful influence in his behalf.

We do not know whether Peter was able to secure the prebend or not. According to Remusat, there was a canon of the cathedral of Nantes who was called Astrolabe. And in the necrology of a Cistercian abbey in Switzerland, according to Cousin, there is mention of an abbot named Astrolabe who presided there between the years 1162 and 1165.

One authority, the English author Enid McLeod, mentions a certain William Abaeler who was a subprior of Argenteuil in 1152, after it had been joined to the monastery of St. Denis, and whose death was recorded under the date of February 27 of that year. Astrolabe could have been using this name.

In the necrology of the Paraclete, under the date of October 30th of that same year, 1152, the death of Astrolabe is recorded with the words, *Petrus Astrolabius magistri nostri Petri filius.* That his death was recorded in the necrology does not necessarily mean that it occurred at the Paraclete.

Actually, all that we have is the fact that Astrolabe was born and the fact that he died. With a fate that is not unusual for a child of illustrious parents, he left nothing else of note for posterity, not even the record of his mother's grief that he should be sacrificed, along with all else, on the altar of her great love for his father.

Heloise lived for twenty-one years after the death of Abelard. If, as she had said, she entered religious orders to please him rather than to please God, one finds, nevertheless, only the highest praise for the way in which she conducted herself and her convent all those years.

Once she had thought that when her husband died she would no longer be able to live. Who has not felt that way who has ever been in love? But Heloise was a woman of strength, both of character and physique. Through her personal grief she learned to sustain an impersonal, unselfish love, and that carried her forward.

The convent of the Paraclete had been Abelard's gift to her. Once it had been a "comforter" to him, and now it was to be that for Heloise. There was plenty of work to be done, and this was perhaps the greatest blessing of all for one who dared not break under the weight of loneliness.

Among the tributes that have been paid to the valiant Heloise, there are these words of Peter, abbot of Cluny:

"I should have shown how large a place of love for you in the Lord I keep in my heart. For truly I do not now first begin to love a person whom I remember that I have loved for a long time. I had not yet completely passed out of adolescence, I had not yet attained young manhood, when the fame, not yet indeed of your religion, but of your distinguished and praiseworthy studies became known to me.

"I heard then that a woman, although she was not yet disentangled from the bonds of the world, devoted the highest zeal to literary studies, which is very unusual, and to the pursuit of wisdom, although it was that of the world. I heard that she could not be hindered by pleasures, frivolities, and delights from this useful pursuit of learning the arts. And when almost everyone is kept from these studies by detestable sloth, and when the progress of wisdom can come to a standstill, I do not say among women, by whom it is entirely rejected, but it is scarcely able to find virile minds among men, you, by your praiseworthy zeal, completely excelled all women, and surpassed almost all men.

"Soon, indeed, according to the words of the apostle, as it pleased Him who brought you forth from your mother's womb to call you by His grace, you exchanged this devotion to studies for a far better one. Now completely and truly a woman of wisdom, you chose the Gospel instead of logic, the apostle in place of physics, Christ instead of Plato, the cloister instead of the academy.

"Now in beginning that which, by divine grace, you will continue well, you have trampled underfoot the ancient serpent always lying in wait for women, and you have so driven it out that it will never dare tempt you further. . . .

"I say these things, dearest sister in the Lord, not indeed to flatter you, but to encourage you, so that, devoting your attention to that great good in which you have for a long time persevered, you may the more ardently continue to serve it carefully, and that you may inflame both by words and example, according to the grace granted to you by God, those holy women who serve the Lord with you, so that they may strive anxiously in this same contest with you. For you, although you are a woman, are one of those creatures whom the prophet Ezekiel saw, who should not only burn like coals of fire, but should glow and shine like lamps.

"You are truly a disciple of truth, but you are also, by that very obligation, inasmuch as it behooves you for those entrusted to you, a mistress of humility. The complete mastery of humility and of all celestial discipline, has been imposed on you by God. Wherefore you ought to take care not only for yourself, but also for the flock entrusted to you, and on behalf of all, you should in all things receive a greater reward.

"Surely the reward of victory awaits you above all, since, as you know best, as many times as the world and the prince of the world have been overcome by your leadership, so many triumphs will be prepared for you with the eternal King and Judge."

The Paraclete by now was so large that it was necessary to divide the property it controlled into no fewer than six daughter houses, which together formed the order of the Paraclete. These were all run by Heloise, in accordance with the rule of St. Benedict, and those special rules she had asked for and received from Abelard. As she grew older and more experienced, Heloise modified these rules to fit the circumstances. She reduced the amount of meat to be eaten by the nuns, and the occasions on which they were to partake of wine. The hours for prayer grew longer, and those for recreation or sleep shorter. Heloise, as she grew older, grew sterner, demanding more of her nuns as she demanded more of herself.

And yet, in spite of the rigor of its rules, the fame of the Paraclete and its abbess drew women to the convent from all over. Among these were many well-born widows and virgins, including the niece of Galo, who continued to make gifts of great value. In addition to members of the great neighboring families, there is a record in the cartulary of the Paraclete of two nieces of Abelard, Agnes and Agathe, one of whom eventually became a prioress there.

Over the next twenty years, the convents that came under the rule of Heloise, in addition to those previously mentioned, were those of Noëfort, St. Flavit, and St. Martin de Boran. With each of these came gifts of money, and sometimes tithes. This meant that, in administering so much wealth, the Abbess Heloise was forced to concern herself more and more with worldly affairs.

There were quarrels about borders which had to be settled, and Heloise occasionally had to travel about to see that they were settled fairly. There were visits that had to be paid regularly to the daughter houses, to make sure that the rules of the order of the Paraclete were scrupulously observed. There were the tithes and other payments that had to be collected, and further gifts to be received from landowners—on which occasions it was necessary for Heloise to show her appreciation by appearing in person when they were bestowed.

But these visits to the world outside were not too frequent, and, such as they were, offered no longer any temptation to the "Lady Heloise," as she was sometimes called. She had reached, as we all must reach someday, the point of no return. The pattern has been set for us, or we have made it ourselves, and there is no longer time, or the energy of youth, or the optimism to change it, or even the wish to change it if we could. For better or for worse, we continue along the path already charted, and if the pattern and the path are good ones, so much the better for us and for the world. So it was now with Heloise, abbess of the Paraclete.

Had she lived more in the world when she was young, had not the whole of her life, except for those few tragic years, been spent behind convent walls, it is reasonable to suppose that Heloise would have left a mark of some kind, anyway, to show that she had existed. Those years of the twelfth century were enormously exciting, with the Holy Wars, the political intrigue, but, above all, with the advancement in poetry, architecture, music, and all fields of knowledge.

Many women managed to come to the fore, especially in the field of political intrigue—women more secure than Heloise by reason of birth and wealth and even beauty. One woman, Eleanor of Aquitaine, wife of two kings and mother of kings and queens, managed to change the history of France and England. What might Heloise, with her richly passionate nature, her brilliant mind, her earthy intelligence, have done had she been free to attend the courts of love, to mingle with the princes of the world, instead of the princes of the church? There is no way of knowing, of course.

But for an intellectual woman, one with a passion for study, the convents of the Middle Ages offered the only opportunity to satisfy her hunger for knowledge, and to advance herself. Perhaps in no other field would Heloise have shone so brilliantly. In the expression of a great and unselfish love, in the embellishment of a great religious order, as well as in the attainments of her extraordinary intellect, Heloise has had few equals.

Did the years pass quickly for Heloise, or did they drag themselves out, those last twenty or twenty-one that represented nearly a third of her life? Was she unconscious of the years—years that have a way of telescoping toward the end, until a year is as a month, a month as a week, a week as a day, and yesterday and tomorrow are as one?

She was a very busy woman. Her days were filled to the brim. Incessant were the demands made upon her as abbess of the order of the Paraclete. And, with unflagging zeal, she gave herself completely to the performance of her duties.

Once she had wanted to know everything there was to be found in books. Once the excitement of a new idea, a new theory, set her on fire, until she had turned it this way and that, followed it through to its logical conclusion, and made it her own or rejected it as false.

Now Heloise accepted what she read: the psalter, the Gospels, the creeds and the chants. She had found a truth that was good to live by, and it was enough for her. The habit she wore was filled a little amply now, as middle age added flesh to her fine bones, but the beauty of face remained. Grace had always been hers, and it could not change or fade. After the busy hours of the day and the early night, there was the silence of her own quarters, and the meditation of her heart to be lived with. It is to

be hoped they brought her peace. Never once had she been willing to believe that God would condemn her for loving Abelard.
But if in God's eyes she had grievously sinned, then she had
atoned for that sin a hundred times over. She had promised
Abelard to pray for him always, and perhaps after the daily
prayers for his soul had been said in the oratory, she offered a
few more of her own before she lay down upon her hard bed to
wait for the mercy of sleep.

The city of Troyes had grown, and the wilderness in which,
years ago, Abelard had built his little oratory, had all but disappeared. Châteaux had risen, with tall slate towers, fortressed
walls, and magnificent banquet halls for the sons of the nobility.
Farms dotted the countryside. Roads had been laid, or had
formed themselves, for the traffic that flowed past the convent
of the Paraclete. And not all of the traffic went by, since there
were many travelers who had reason to stop at the gate and
demand admittance of the porteress.

Townspeople called to consult the abbess about family
troubles. Parents of daughters who had not married, or would
not marry, came to discuss the subject of vocation. And there
were others, widows or those who had griefs to overcome, who
begged for admission, and offered both themselves and their
private fortunes to the convent and the church if the abbess
would admit them to the order.

Tradespeople came with things to sell or exchange, neighbors
appeared with gifts for the nuns, or with grievances about some
encroachment of their property, or with disputes among themselves that they wished the abbess, in her wisdom, to arbitrate.
Recently bereaved parents or husbands or wives called to be
comforted and to ask that prayers be said for their dead. The
abbess saw all of these, and comforted, advised, or reproved
them.

There were dignitaries too, who came with their retinues.
These were received with formality and the best the convent
had to offer in the way of fowls from the barnyard, freshly
churned butter, and bread that was freshly baked in the convent

ovens. They were also offered wine that had been pressed from the grapes in the vineyards that adjoined the Paraclete.

As the need arose, the abbess set forth, with suitable companions, to pay a visit of her own, to insure the proper filling out of a charter, to obtain a favor from an archbishop for the good of the Paraclete and its daughter convents.

Did she always enjoy that splendid vitality which made her able to accomplish feats that would have wearied strong men? Did she begin to tire at the end, and to suffer from the illnesses to which the flesh seems heir? There is no record.

Nothing is known of the way in which Heloise died, or of the cause of her death. There is even some discrepancy in the dates that have been handed down to us. Some authorities give the year as 1163, others the year 1164. But the day of the month, as recorded in the necrology of the Paraclete, is May 16. Tradition has it, however, that she was sixty-three, the same age as Abelard when he died.

There is a brief entry in the book of sepulchers of the Paraclete: "Helevis, first abbess of the *Petit Moustier*"—which is how the oratory Abelard built was afterward called.

A contemporary, William Godel, recorded that she was buried before the altar, as was Abelard. Her epitaph, which was preserved, reads as follows:

"*Hoc tumulo abbatissa jacet prudens Heloissa*
Paraclitum statuit, cum Paraclito requiescit.
Gaudia sanctorum sua sunt super alta polorum,
Nos meritis precibusque suis exalter ab imis."

(Here in this tomb lies the wise Heloise.
She established the Paraclete and with the Paraclete
    now rests.
The joys of the saints are now hers in the highest heaven,
May we be exalted from the depths by her merits.)

And the nuns of the Paraclete, who knew her and loved her, left this record of her passing: "Heloise, the first abbess and mother of our religion, most famous for her learning and piety, departed happily to the Lord."

Did those same nuns, who sat by Heloise as she lay dying, carry out the rule as given by Abelard, sending one of their members from the sickbed to beat upon a board and thus summon the other nuns? And did the rest come running on silent feet through the damp corridors, beginning the litany and murmuring the invocation of the saints, male and female, until they reached the bedside of their abbess? Was there a priest among them to say, as Abelard himself had suggested, "It is better to go to the house of mourning than to go to a house of feasting: for that is the end of all men; and the living will lay it to his heart."

One may be sure that Heloise had strength enough at the end to insist that all of Abelard's rules be observed, and that, seeing this done, she "departed happily to the Lord."

Straightway then, the sisters, as was also written in Abelard's rule, deeply grieved and weeping, washed the body of their abbess and wrapped it tenderly in a shroud that, because of her exalted position, completely covered her. After which, Heloise received no other honor than to be buried as were the lowliest of her nuns.

In the chronicle of St. Martin of Tours, this legend appears: that, as Heloise was lying in her last illness, she directed that after her death she should be laid in the tomb of Abelard. And, when her dead body was carried to the open tomb, her husband raised his arms to receive her, "and so embracing her, closed them fast around her."

The legend, for what it is worth, belongs to the Middle Ages. But it is true that for eight hundred years or so, since they were placed in a single grave, Heloise and Abelard have remained side by side, united in death.

The number of times, however, that their relics were moved makes a story in itself. While it may be macabre, it adds a touch of symbolism and beauty to the romance of those "star-crossed lovers," as Helen Waddell called them.

For three hundred years they lay in a single crypt in the oratory of the Paraclete. Then, in 1497, when Catherine de Courcelles was abbess, she had the bodies exhumed and buried in the church of the Paraclete, which was on higher ground. Here they were separated, in a sense, but only by the high altar, Abelard having been placed on the right of it and Heloise on the left.

In 1621, when Marie de la Rochefoucald, the first of that distinguished family to enter the convent of the Paraclete, became its abbess, she had the remains of Abelard and Heloise placed in a single crypt beneath the high altar. Thus they remained until the year 1768, when the prioress, Genevieve du Passage, with the consent of the community, had the bones verified by two surgeons, in the presence of two officers of justice. This, apparently, was the first time the relics were examined.

In 1780, the Abbess Marie-Charlotte de la Rochefoucald, incidentally the last abbess of the Paraclete, had the remains moved again to the other end of the same crypt, also before witnesses. The curé of Quincey, who presided at this occasion, left an account of what was found. He related that the bones were well preserved in spite of the dampness to which they had been exposed during the time they remained in the crypt of the *Petit Moustier* by the river Arduson. Another eyewitness related, however, that "the bones of Abelard were almost entirely reduced to powder with the exception of the skull . . . but that the bones of Heloise were remarkably preserved."

At this same ceremony, there was provided a tomb of black marble on which was engraved the following epitaph:

> *Hic*
> *Suh eodem marmore jacent*
> *Hujus monasterii*
> *Conditor Petrus Abaelardus*
> *Et Abbatissa prima Heloissa;*
> *Olim studiis, engenio, amore, infaustis nuptiis*
> *Et poenitentia*

Nunc aeterna, quod speramus, felicitate
Conjuncti
Petris obiit xx *prima Aprilis anno* MXXLII
Heloissa, XVII *Mai* MCLXIII.
Curis Carolae de Roucy Paracleti abbatissae
M.DCC.LXXX.

Twelve years after this ceremony, necessity made the removal of the remains no longer merely a matter of suitability or ritual. All of France was trembling on the verge of the revolution. Before it began, an artist named Lenoir, fearing that all trace of the lovers whose story had greatly moved him would be lost, quickly made a sketch of the tomb and of the statue of the Trinity which now adorned it, and presented the sketch to the Louvre along with the rest of his drawings.

When the revolution did break out, among the first victims were the convents and monasteries. On November 14, 1792, the Paraclete was sold by the state, and the convent and nearly all its buildings were destroyed. (Oddly enough, a small building was saved. This was one that had been used as a private dwelling by the last abbess. It became the home of a succession of families and exists today.)

A few days before the sale, several citizens of Nogent exhumed the bodies of Abelard and Heloise and had them reverently placed in a crypt in the Chapel of St. Leger of the Church of St. Laurent, in Nogent. In spite of the danger to those who attended it, a ceremony was held at the time, and later a copper inscription was placed on the wall to commemorate the event.

According to the devoted artist Lenoir, who attended the ceremony, and may have inspired it, the bones of Abelard showed him to have been tall and strong, and those of Heloise were also of beautiful proportions. "The skull of Heloise," he added, perhaps with a bit of fantasy, "expressed a perfect beauty!"

The temper of the time was not one of veneration for relics, religious or otherwise, yet Lenoir was not intimidated. He had no intention of letting the precious remains of Heloise and Abe-

lard suffer the same fate that befell the statue of the Trinity on
their tomb, which had been smashed by a group of iconoclasts
in 1794. He opened a museum, in about 1798, for the preservation and display of French *"monuments historiques."* He respect-
fully requested of the authorities the remains of Heloise and
Abelard for burial in a *champs elysées* that he planned to construct in the garden of the museum, and which was to contain
the tombs of famous French men and women.

While he was waiting for the relics to be given into his custody,
Lenoir somehow managed to have casts made of the skulls, from
which the sculptor Deseine made busts. He then acquired a stone
sarcophagus which was said to come from the monastery of St.
Marcel, where Abelard died and which was believed to be the
one in which he had first been buried. The figure of a monk
which decorated the lid of the sarcophagus was said to be a
statue of Abelard. Into this sarcophagus, in the year 1802,
Lenoir placed the remains of Abelard and Heloise, with an
effigy of Heloise on the lid beside that of Abelard.

Lenoir then had a chapel built in the *elysées*, supposedly in
twelfth-century style, but actually Gothic. To adorn it he used
two medallions representing the lovers, and around the base of
a column which supported the tomb, he carved the names of
Abelard and Heloise. Trees were planted about the little shrine,
which became a favorite spot for the sight-seers whom Lenoir
welcomed.

In October, 1814, Lenoir's land was ceded to the city of Paris
for a cemetery, and the museum was closed by government
decree. Lenoir made a plea that the ashes of Heloise and Abelard be spared the fate of the other celebrities, and it was decided
that they should be placed together in the cemetery of Mont-
Louis, which is now called Père-Lachaise. The removal was accomplished with a great deal of ceremony. The biers were conducted with all the elegance of a French *pompe funèbre du
première classe,* to the church of St. Germain-des-Prés, in Mont-
parnasse, where a high mass was said over them. They were
then stored in a room of the house that had belonged to the
Jesuit, La Chaise, the confessor of Louis XIV.

Five months later, the biers were carried to the monument which was constructed for them in the cemetery, and there they remain today. In 1913 the original epitaph was carved anew in white marble, and the inscription added that the tomb contains the remains of Abelard and Heloise. Time and the elements have almost obliterated the dates.

In the sentimental period at the end of the last century, the enthusiasm of the crowds of lovers who made pilgrimages to the tomb made it necessary to erect a protective iron fence around it. Now, in our more cynical age, visitors are scarcer, and the tomb has a rather neglected air. Yet, in spite of that, it manages to preserve a certain dignity and grandeur.

Heloise and Abelard, may they rest in peace! The world has troubled them enough, in life and after death, giving them no rest. In the words of Isaiah: "the works of righteousness shall be peace: and the affect of righteousness quietness and assurance for ever."

The Scriptures have also promised that "the last enemy that shall be destroyed is death."

Surely, however great was the sin that Heloise and Abelard shared and for which they atoned separately, it was forgiven by the One they so faithfully served. And surely in them the promise of the Scriptures has been met, and the last enemy overcome by love, that is stronger and more lasting, even, than death!

BIBLIOGRAPHY

PETRI ABAELARDI—OPERA OMNIA; Paris: Migne, 1885.

ABELARD ET HELOISE by M. & Mme. Guizot. Paris: Didier, 1853.

HISTORIA CALAMITATUM by Pierre Abelard. Trans. by Henry Adams Bellows. Glencoe, Ill.: Free Press, 1958. (Reprint.)

THE LETTERS OF ABELARD AND HELOISE, trans. by C. K. Scott Moncrieff. New York: Knopf, 1926.

LETTERS OF ABELARD AND ELOISA by John Hughes, Esq., with poems by Mr. Pope and others. Philadelphia: printed by C. Whittingham, 1824.

REALISM AND NOMINALISM by Meyrick H. Carre. London: Oxford University Press, 1946.

ORIGIN OF UNIVERSITIES by Gabriel Compayre. New York: Scribners, 1893.

HELOISE À ARGENTEUIL by Etienne Henry Gilson. Paris: J. Vrin, 1938.

HELOISE, A BIOGRAPHY by Enid McLeod. London: Chatto and Windus, 1938.

ABELARD PIERRE by C. de Remusat. Paris: Didier, 1855.

THE ROMANCE OF ABELARD AND HELOISE by Orlando Williams Wight. New York: Appleton, 1853.

DEUX COUVENS AU MOYENAGE: St. Gildas et le Paraclet by Paul Tiby. Paris: 1851.

HELOISE AND ABELARD, a novel by George Moore. New York: Boni & Liveright, 1921.

PETER ABELARD, a novel by Helen Jane Waddell. New York: Henry Holt, 1933.

THE WANDERING SCHOLARS by Helen Waddell. New York: Doubleday Anchor Books, 1955. (Reprint.)

FROM RITUAL TO ROMANCE by Jessie L. Weston. New York: Doubleday, 1957. (Reprint.)

MEDIEVAL PEOPLE by Eileen Power. New York: Doubleday Anchor Books, (Reprint.)

PHILOSOPHY AND CIVILIZATION IN THE MIDDLE AGES by Maurice de Wulf. Princeton University Press, 1922.

MONT-SAINT-MICHEL-AND-CHARTRES by Henry Adams. New York: Doubleday Anchor Books, 1959. (Reprint.)

THE STORY OF FRANCE by Thomas E. Watson. New York: Macmillan, 1904.

AN OUTLINE OF FRENCH HISTORY by Rene Sedillet. New York: Knopf, 1953.

THE AENEID by Vergil. Trans. by W. Jackson Knight. New York: Penquin Classics, 1956. (Reprint.)

THE MEDIEVAL MIND by Henry Osborn Taylor. New York: Macmillan, 1919.

WARRIORS OF GOD by Walter Migg. New York: Knopf, 1959.

WORKS OF THE ENGLISH POETS, Vol. 65, by Samuel Johnson. (Morgan Library)

EPISTLE ELOISA TO ABELARD by Alexander Pope. Bibliophile Society, 1923.

A SURVEY OF EUROPEAN CIVILIZATION by Ferguson Bruun. New York: Houghton Mifflin, 1958.

UNIVERSITIES OF EUROPE IN THE MIDDLE AGES by H. Rashdale. Oxford, 1895.

ST. BENEDICT by St. Gregory. Trans. by Abbot McCann. Worcester, England: Stanbrook Abbey Press.

THE RULE OF ST. BENEDICT, trans. by Abbot McCann. London: Burns Oates, 1952.

A HISTORY OF BENEDICTINE NUNS by S. Hilpisch. Collegeville, Minn: Abbey Press, 1958.

JUBILEE, a magazine, issue of May, 1959.

HISTORIC COSTUME by Lucy Barton. Boston: Walter Baker Co., 1938.

THE MEDIEVAL READER, edited by Ross and McLaughlin. New York: Viking, 1949.

HISTORIA PROLIFICUS, edited by R. L. Poole. Oxford: Clarendon Press, 1927.

THE CLOISTERS by James J. Rorimer. New York: Metropolitan Museum of Art, 1951.

CATECHISME DU DIOCESE DE CAHORS, edited by Etienne Delsaud. Cahors, France: 1912.